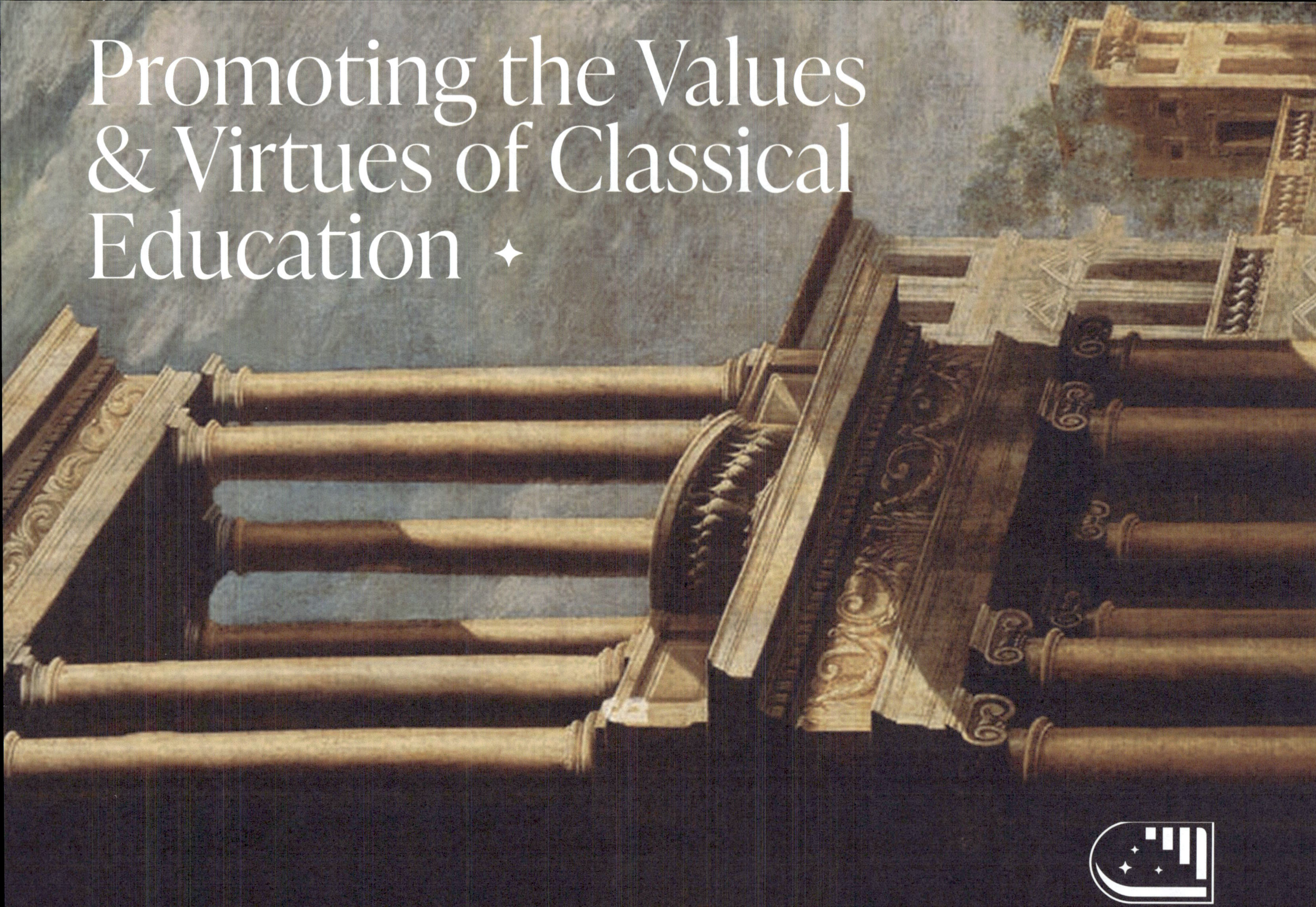
Promoting the Values
& Virtues of Classical
Education

THALES PRESS

LEVEL 2.0

Write in the Middle

A Workbook for Junior High Students

Volume I

Thales Press Raleigh, North Carolina

This book is the property of:

***Thales Trivium:* Write in the Middle, Volume I**

***Thales Trivium:* Write in the Middle, Volume I** was published in Raleigh, North Carolina for use in Thales Academy, a network of low-cost, high-quality private schools in North Carolina, South Carolina, Tennessee, and Virginia.

All photos, unless otherwise noted, are available in the public domain.

Thales Press would like to thank and acknowledge the work of Elizabeth Jetton, the primary author of this workbook.

Special thanks to Brett Martinez, Ali Graziosi, Hannah Breeding, and Andrew Roberts for their advice and contributions to this work.

For more information and supplementary resources that include pacing guides, assessments, project ideas, and other elements, email us at ***thalespress@thalesacademy.org***

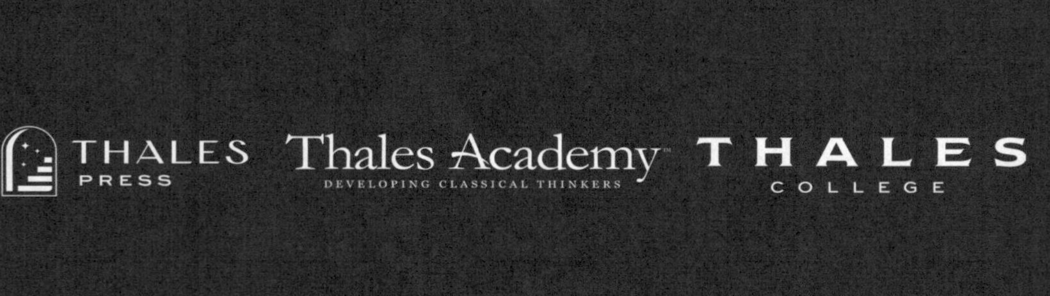

Table of Contents

Introduction to Writing

CLEAR AND EFFECTIVE written communication is incredibly important. From emailing a friend to crafting a research paper, writing well is essential to success. As a middle school student, you will learn to formulate good ideas, support those ideas with strong evidence, and eloquently present those ideas to your given audience. Below are some of the concepts you will be learning:

1. Thesis Statements
2. Outlines
3. Paragraphs
4. Word Choice
5. Sentence Structure
6. Types of Essays
7. Researching and Evaluating Sources
8. Paraphrasing and Citations

Learning to Write

Learning to write is very different from learning most other subjects. In most subjects, there is a right or wrong answer. Sometimes those answers are more complicated than others or take longer to figure out, but ultimately, there is only one correct answer. In writing, there is much more variation. As early as kindergarten, you could probably write a sentence. By the time you finished third grade, you could probably write a basic essay. However, just because an essay has the correct number of sentences and is grammatically correct, does not mean that it is a quality essay or that it will earn a good grade. Every essay is different, even ones written in response to the same **prompt**, which makes it difficult to learn how to write one well.

Think about it this way. If you are instructed to write an essay about your life, each of you will have a very different response. One student who has lived in the same house her whole life and spends most of her afternoons and weekends practicing and competing in gymnastics may write extensively about one subject, namely her days as a gymnast and what that entails. A second student who has lived in multiple different countries and never stayed in the same town more than one year might write an essay composed of multiple shorter paragraphs detailing the differences in his life in each new country. Your teacher may provide you guidance regarding the expected number of sentences or paragraphs, especially early on, but it is up to you to come up with your reasons and explanations in support of your ideas. Your ideas are just that – yours

Every essay is different, even ones written in response to the same prompt, which makes it difficult to learn how to write one well. Essays will generally consist of an introduction, a body, and a conclusion.

Vocabulary

Prompt
The directions of an essay assignment that provides a question to answer or other guidance on what to write about.

Essay
A piece of work that discusses one main topic. It begins with an introduction and ends with a conclusion.

Introduction
The first paragraph of an essay that grabs the reader's attention and presents what the essay is about.

Conclusion
The last paragraph of an essay that sums up everything that was stated and provides a sense of closure to the essay.

FRANCIS BACON
British Statesman, 1561–1626, often seen as the father of the English essay.

– and your teacher cannot come up with them for you. And, as your get older, teachers will provide you with less and less specific guidance, instead leaving it up to you to craft an essay that is well-written and explained, divided into the appropriate number of paragraphs to justify or explain your particular idea.

What Is an Essay?

Future chapters will go into detail on each element of an essay; however, it is important that you have a basic understanding of what an essay is before we discuss each element in turn. An **essay** is a piece of writing made up of multiple sentences and paragraphs about one particular topic. Essays can vary in length from one paragraph to dozens of pages, but one thing is always the same: it will begin with an **introduction** that grabs the reader's attention and presents what the essay is about, and it will end with a **conclusion** that sums up everything that was stated and provides a sense of closure to the essay. Between the introduction and conclusion, you will have a varying number of sentences and paragraphs where you present your information or argument. Every essay you write will differ, and it is up to you to write the best one you can each time.

ESSAY

Journal Writing / Practice Makes Perfect

What do you find difficult about writing? Go into detail, explaining what you find difficult and why you think you find this area difficult. Remember, everyone is different. Maybe you find only one area difficult, maybe you find three or four areas difficult. Your response should be at least five sentences long, and if you are only writing about one area, you should discuss it in more detail than if you are talking about multiple areas. Be sure to begin your writing with a general opening sentence and end with a concluding sentence.

ESSAY

Writing is Rewriting / Revising

A major part of the writing process is revising your work. You may have typos where you simply left a letter off of a word, or you may realize that one of your paragraphs doesn't support your point as well as you thought. Maybe after letting it sit, you realize you need more evidence for one of your points. Your job is to take your journal entry on the previous page and revise and rewrite it. Check for any grammatical errors, add more details, remove irrelevant information, and so forth. Write your final response below. Your resulting piece will most likely be longer than your original one.

MOUNTAINS, WATERCOLOR LANDSCAPE

Artwork by Hanna

Section I
Prewriting

CHAPTERS

01 Brainstorming

02 Thesis Statements

03 Essay Maps & Outlines

LIGHT WATERCOLOR OF HIGH MOUNTAINS

Prewriting is the very beginning of the writing process. It sets the scene, gives you ideas of what to write about, and helps you determine where to begin.

Artwork by Ramon Grosso

CHAPTER

Brainstorming

ROADMAP

- Learn about the very first steps of writing an essay.
- Discuss brainstorming techniques.
- Practice coming up with good ideas based on prompts.

THALES OUTCOME

Nº 5

A **Critical Thinker** *discerns the truth of a statement or observation through questioning and examination.*

When beginning to write, the first step is to think critically about the prompt or topic of the assignment. By thinking critically about the assigned issue, you will be able to generate a variety of quality ideas to include in your essay and create a compelling argument.

Brainstorming & Prewriting

ONCE YOU HAVE RECEIVED a writing assignment, your first job is to begin **prewriting**. Prewriting is the process of coming up with and writing down ideas related to the topic. There are many ways to begin prewriting. You might free write, where you write as many ideas as you can down on your paper, or you might create a brainstorming web where you write out a bunch of interconnected ideas. When you are prewriting, you often list many more ideas than you need to include, and then you go back and reduce it to a few main points that will become the body of your essay.

If your assignment requires you to conduct research, you will want to begin the research process first. You cannot list reasons why Martin Luther King, Jr. was an inspiring leader or how music effects the brain if you have not first researched these concepts. For assignments that require research, first read about your topic and take notes, then organize that information into groups that could become your main reasons. Research papers will be discussed in more detail in Chapter 12.

If your assignment does not require research, simply begin writing ideas on paper. In a **brainstorming web**, put the topic of your essay at the center of your paper. Branching off from the center, list as many reasons as you can. Add details to those reasons by adding additional branches.

Imagine you have been give the prompt *Write a four-paragraph essay on someone you admire and explain why you admire that person.* The next page shows a sample brainstorming web based on this prompt. Notice how the center of the web is the person the author admires, in this case, *Dad*. Then, jutting out from that central choice are a variety of reasons he is admired. The author lists six different traits she admires: ***plays guitar***, ***kind***, ***smart***, ***organized***, ***supportive***, and ***positive attitude***. Connected to those reasons are details describing each of those traits. When brainstorming, add as much as you can think of. Remember, not all the information will end up in your essay. This exercise is a chance to get all your ideas together on paper in order to help you consolidate your ideas into a few main points.

Before beginning to write the essay itself, you must spend time thinking about and brainstorming your topic in order to organize your ideas into strong main points.

Vocabulary

Write down this vocabulary in your notebook. These terms will help you better learn and understand the material in this chapter.

Prewriting
The process of coming up with and writing down ideas relating to a topic in preparation for writing an essay or similar piece of work.

Brainstorming Web
A visual way of writing down your ideas in which you place the main idea at the center of your web and list many connected ideas off of that.

The next step after creating a detailed brainstorming web is to narrow those ideas down to a few main points. Choose your strongest points and eliminate the weaker ones. For a four-paragraph essay, you would choose two main points. An essay usually has an introduction and conclusion as its first and last paragraph, leaving two body paragraphs each composed of one main idea (these different paragraphs will be discussed in more detail in subsequent chapters). Using the web above, if this were a four-paragraph assignment, you might choose ***kind*** and ***supportive*** as your main points. If the assignment were to write a five-paragraph essay (meaning you need three main points) you might choose ***kind***, ***supportive***, and ***smart***, though you might need to brainstorm a little more to expand your thoughts on ***smart***.

Once you have chosen which main ideas to focus on, you will want to write your thesis and organize your ideas into a prewriting map or outline, which will be discussed in the next chapter.

ACTIVITY

Brainstorming Web / Practice 1

Create a brainstorming web for the following research-free prompt: ***Think about a person you admire. Why do you admire them?***

Brainstorming Space:

ACTIVITY

Brainstorming Web / Practice 2

Create a brainstorming web for the following research-free prompt: ***Which season is your favorite? Explain why it is your favorite.***

Brainstorming Space:

ACTIVITY

Brainstorming Web / Practice 3

Create a brainstorming web for the following research-free prompt: ***What makes you happy?***

Brainstorming Space:

ACTIVITY

Brainstorming Web / Practice 4

Create a brainstorming web for the following research-free prompt: ***What are the characteristics and habits of a successful student?***

Brainstorming Space:

ACTIVITY

Brainstorming Web / Research Practice 1

You will be creating a brainstorming web for the following research prompt: ***What are the benefits of learning a foreign language?*** Remember, for a research prompt, you will first need to research and take notes on the topic, so in the space below, write your notes from your research, and on the next page, create your brainstorming web.

Link to resource used:	
Author:	
Title:	

Notes:

Link to resource used:	
Author:	
Title:	

Notes:

ACTIVITY

Brainstorming Web / Research Practice 1

Now, create a brainstorming web for ***What are the benefits of learning a foreign language?*** based on your research notes on the previous page.

Brainstorming Space:

ACTIVITY

Brainstorming Web / Research Practice 2

You will be creating a brainstorming web for the following research prompt: ***Why should every student study the fine arts?*** Remember, for a research prompt, you will first need to research and take notes on the topic, so in the space below, write your notes from your research, and on the next page, create your brainstorming web.

Link to resource used:	
Author:	
Title:	

Notes:

Link to resource used:	
Author:	
Title:	

Notes:

ACTIVITY

Brainstorming Web / Research Practice 2

Now, create a brainstorming web for ***Why should every student study the fine arts?*** based on your research notes on the previous page.

Brainstorming Space:

ACTIVITY

Brainstorming Web / Research Practice 3

You will be creating a brainstorming web for the following research prompt: ***What are the benefits of participating in a study abroad program?*** Remember, for a research prompt, you first need to research and take notes on the topic, so in the space below, write your notes from your research, and on the next page, create your brainstorming web.

Link to resource used:	
Author:	
Title:	

Notes:

Link to resource used:	
Author:	
Title:	

Notes:

ACTIVITY

Brainstorming Web / Research Practice 3

Now, create a brainstorming web for *What are the benefits of participating in a study abroad program?* based on your research notes on the previous page.

Brainstorming Space:

Essay

Creative Writing / Practice Makes Perfect

Remember, the more you write, the better you'll get. Let's have some fun writing on the following if/then question. You can write it as a story, a descriptive essay, or in the form of an encyclopedia entry as if you are a scientist. First, brainstorm your ideas below so you have an idea of what you are going to write about before you begin.

What if you walked out your front door one day and discovered a working time-travel machine in your front yard?

Brainstorming Space:

ESSAY

Creative Writing / Practice Makes Perfect

Now that you have brainstormed some of your ideas and know where your story is headed, answer the prompt in complete sentences in the space provided. You can write it as a story, a descriptive essay, or in the form of an encyclopedia entry as if you are a scientist. When you are done, go back and reread your work and revise for typos and grammar errors, and with your teacher's permission, share it with a classmate.

What if you walked out your front door one day and discovered a working time-travel machine in your front yard?

ESSAY

Essay

LIGHT WATERCOLOR OF HIGH MOUNTAINS

Your thesis statement is the road map of your essay. It shows your reader the path they will take and what to expect, much like this road winding through the mountains.

Painting by Ramon Grosso

CHAPTER 2

Thesis Statements

ROADMAP

- Learn about the elements of a strong thesis statement.
- Practice writing thesis statements.

THALES OUTCOME
Nº 8

Astute Problem Solving *leads one to identify the solutions to a problem, evaluate likely outcomes, assess risk, and choose correctly.*

The next phase of essay writing involves analyzing your prewriting map and choosing the strongest, most compelling reasons to support your main idea. Astute problem solving will enable you to narrow down your web of ideas in order to formulate your thesis statement.

Thesis Statements

CREATING A STRONG THESIS statement is one of the most essential skills to writing an essay. A **thesis statement** is one to two sentences that presents the claim that you plan to argue for in your essay. It also usually contains the main points that you will use to support that claim (the statement of main points is also known separately as the **advance organizer**). The thesis is usually located at the end of your introduction, which we will discuss in the next chapter.

Think of your thesis as the roadmap of your essay. A reader should be able to tell exactly what your essay will prove just by reading these one or two sentences. This means that you need to first brainstorm (and research, if necessary) your topic before you can begin crafting your thesis. If you do not know where your argument will lead, how can you draw a map for your reader?

Once you have spent time brainstorming your topic, you are ready to begin formulating your thesis. Your thesis should clearly identify the topic, your point of view, and the main ways you plan to prove or explain that point of view. For example, imagine you were given the prompt *Should schools follow the traditional or year-round calendar?* First, you would brainstorm your topic, most likely listing out several reasons for and against both calendars. Then, you would analyze your notes and see which side has more support. That determines your point of view on your topic — what side of the argument you will support. Lastly, you would use your brainstorming notes to narrow your ideas down into a few main reasons to support that side. After all that, you would give a concise thesis statement that shows the readers what your essay will prove and how you will prove it. It may say *The year-round calendar is better than the traditional calendar because it reduces vacation crowds, decreases lost learning, and improves student attitudes.* On the other hand, perhaps you took the other side of the argument and stated *The traditional calendar is more convenient for parents, more fun for students, and easier for family get-togethers. Therefore, it is superior to the year-round calendar.* Notice how both of these statements make clear which side the author will be supporting and the main reasons he or she will use to get there, providing us, the readers, with a map to follow as we read the rest of the essay.

Overall, to be a quality thesis statement, it needs to be *clear*, *debatable*, and *organized*. Let's go further in depth about each of these areas.

A thesis statement is one to two sentences that clearly show what the essay will argue and the main reasons the author will use to prove it.

Vocabulary

Thesis Statement
One to two sentences that present the claim that you plan to argue for in your essay. It should clearly identify the topic, your point of view, and the main ways you plan to prove or explain that point of view.

Advance Organizer
A brief list of the main points you will use to prove the claim of your thesis. It is often presented as a list within the thesis statement but can also be its own sentence directly after the thesis.

Thesis Must Be Clear

It is essential that your thesis is clear. Your thesis must plainly show the side that you are arguing for. In other words, it cannot make a claim for both sides or merely present the general topic. Not only will an unclear thesis be difficult for your reader to understand or follow along with for the rest of your essay, but it will also make your essay more difficult to write. As you write the rest of your essay, you should always keep that thesis statement in mind to ensure that you do not get led off course by other ideas that are not related to your main argument.

Unclear	Clear
Some people feel that having students learn a foreign language in school is important to being successful in the global marketplace. However, others think it is a useless skill and should not be mandatory. *This presents both possible sides and does not make clear what side you are arguing for.*	Learning a foreign language is a vital skill to compete in the global world. Therefore, children should have to go through foreign language education throughout their school years. *This thesis clearly shows what side you will be arguing for.*

Thesis Must Be Debatable

In general, a thesis statement must be debatable in some way. This means that it is something someone can argue for (or against). Even informative essays should be guided by a debatable thesis statement. In the case of a more informative topic, think of choosing a thesis that needs elaboration. A statement of fact is not debatable and does not need elaboration and therefore cannot be a thesis.

Not Debatable	Debatable
Ebooks are becoming more popular in society. *This is just a fact. Simply presenting a statistic can show whether ebooks are getting more popular. This is not something that someone can argue for or against, and therefore it is not debatable*	Ebooks have several inherent benefits which are leading to their increased popularity over hard copy books. *This is a quality thesis because the reason they are getting more popular is something that can be debated.*

Not Debatable	Debatable
My dad is an engineer. *This sentence is just a fact and does not clearly state what you will be arguing for or telling us about. This is not something that someone can argue against, and therefore it is not debatable.*	My dad is a successful engineer because he works hard and is always learning new things. *This is a quality thesis because it is clear what you will be explaining, and the reason he is successful is something that can be debated and therefore needs more explanation.*

Thesis Must Be Organized & Grammatically Correct

To help keep your essay organized, the thesis will often contain an advance organizer, the list of the main reasons you will use to support your claim. Later we will learn how each of those main reasons becomes a body paragraph of your essay. Whenever you have a list of items, phrases, or clauses within a sentence, you must use **parallel language**. Parallel language refers to using the same part of speech and structure for each item in a list. Your advance organizer can be added to your thesis statement as part of the same sentence, or it can be an additional sentence after the thesis statements. Either way, you must use parallel language in order to have a grammatically correct sentence.

Not Parallel	Parallel
My favorite summer activities are to go hiking, spending time at the pool, and I like to go biking. *Notice how "to go hiking," "spending time at the pool," and "I like to go biking" are all different forms (an infinitive, a gerund, and a clause, respectively).*	My favorite summer activities are hiking, swimming, and biking. My favorite season is summer. I find it especially enjoyable because I can hike in the woods, cool off in the pool, and go biking with my family. *For each list, the structure matches. Notice how the lists can be composed of single words or even full clauses, but within each sentence, they need to be in the same form such as all "-ing" verbs or all nouns.*

Word Choice

Although your thesis is something you write to show your reader what your essay will discuss, and it often contains an opinion, the sentences should not contain words like *I* or *me* unless you are writing a narrative essay like the sample above, and they should never contain references to your reader or to

A·Z

Vocabulary

Parallel Language
Using the same part of speech and structure for each item, phrase, or clause in a list within a single sentence.

First Person Pronouns
Pronouns that include the speaker such as "I," "me," "my," "we," and "us."

Second Person Pronouns
Pronouns directed at the audience your are speaking to. It includes the pronouns "you," "your," and "yours."

Imperative Sentence
A sentence that makes a command and uses the implied pronoun *you*.

the fact that you are writing an essay about a topic. As a result, you should avoid words like *you*, *think*, *essay*, *show*, *tell* etc. Words like these weaken your sentence and make you sound less confident in your ideas. Your thesis should not say *This essay will tell you why cats are better than dogs* or *I think that cats are better than dogs.* We already know that you think it and that you are writing an essay, so these phrases only make you sound unsure of your topic. Instead, a strong thesis would say *Cats are better than dogs because they are independent, quiet, and easy to care for.* Notice how this thesis clearly and confidently declares your point of view and shows us the main ideas you will discuss in the remainder of your essay without any need for *I* or *you*.

These types of pronouns are known as first and second person pronouns. **First person pronouns** are pronouns that include the speaker, like *I*, *me*, or *us*.

Second person pronouns are ones that refer to the audience you are speaking to, like *you* and *yours*. Generally, a thesis (and the rest of the essay as well) should be written in third person point of view. Third person pronouns are ones that refer to other people or things like *they*, *he*, or *it*. Writing in the first or second person is more informal and should not be used in formal essays.

You should also keep in mind that **imperative sentences** are second person sentences because they have the implied pronoun *you*. These are sentences that make a command like *Pay close attention to your thesis statement*. These sentences use second person and thus should be avoided in your formal essays as well.

See the charts below for the different pronouns, followed by some sample incorrect and correct thesis statements.

First Person	Second Person	Third Person
I me mine *us we our ours*	*You your yours*	*it its he she* *his her hers* *they them their theirs*

Incorrect	Correct
In this essay, I will argue about why ebooks are popular. You should get an ebook because they are convenient and have many unique features. I think everyone should use ebooks because they are convenient and have many unique features. *These all contain unnecessary first or second person point of view and none of them are narrative essays.*	Ebooks are gaining in popularity because they are convenient and have many unique features. Ebooks are better than print books because they are convenient and have many unique features. *Any one of the theses (the plural of "thesis") presented on the left could have been worded like the ones above. Each thesis above clearly shows the goal of the essay and is written solely in the third person point of view.*

We should note, though, that some essay prompts are specifically narrative in nature, including the prompt from Chapter 1 about a person you admire. It is permissible to use first person point of view if the essay is personal or autobiographical. A good rule is that if the prompt for the essay is to write something about yourself, first person point of view may be allowed. Keep in mind that you should not use *I* in your thesis even if a prompt asks you to express an opinion. Persuasive essays are all based on choosing a side, but your thesis should still be written in the third person.

Incorrect	Correct
I am going to tell you about my favorite activities which are hiking, swimming, and biking. This essay is about why soccer is my favorite activity. *These all contain unnecessary first person pronouns or references to the writing of the essay itself which only serve to weaken the thesis statement.*	My favorite activities are hiking, biking, and swimming. I have many activities that I enjoy, but my favorites by far are hiking, biking, and swimming. *In spite of the fact that these thesis statements contain first person pronouns, these are quality theses because first person pronouns are all necessary to the topic of the essay which is your own personal favorite activities.*

Putting it all together

Let us return to our sample prompt from earlier: *Write an essay about a person you admire*. In Chapter 1, we created this brainstorming web:

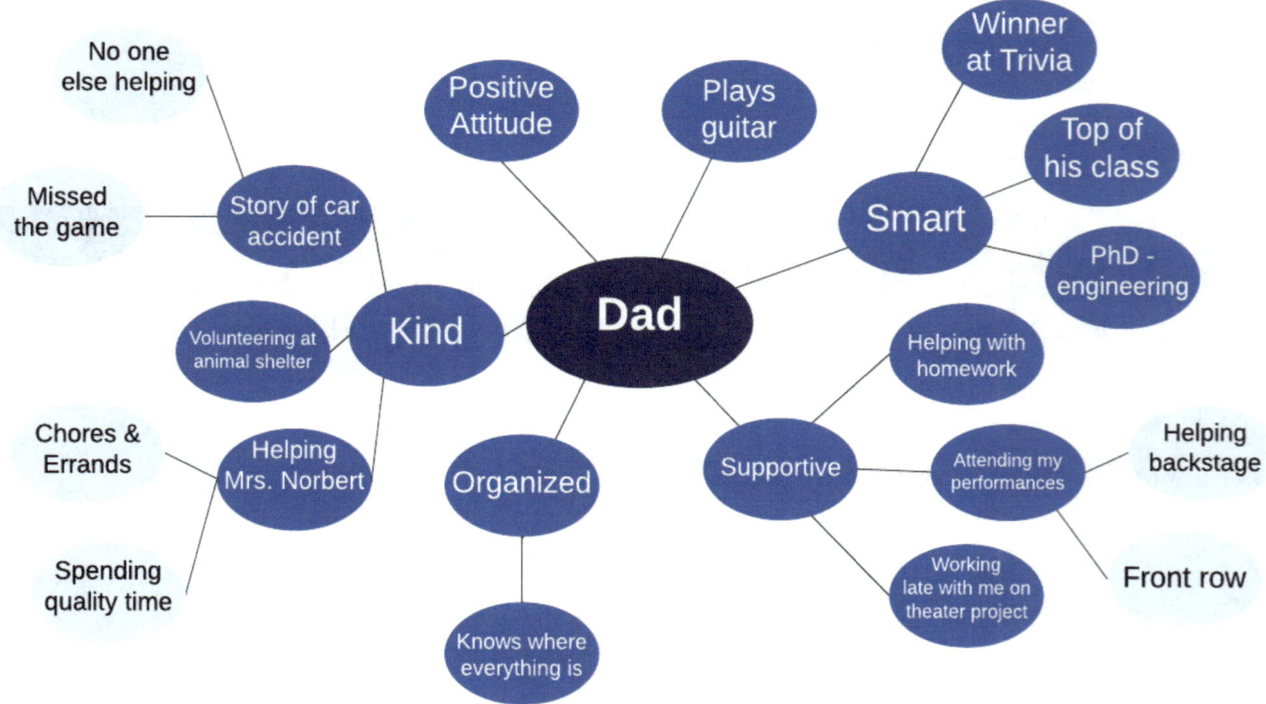

We can see that we had the most ideas about the concepts *kind* and *supportive*, closely followed by *smart*. Based on the requirements of the essay such as the number of main points or paragraphs, our thesis might be ***I admire my father because he is kind to everyone and supportive of all my endeavors*** or ***I admire my father because he is smart, kind, and supportive.*** Notice that first person point of view is acceptable for this thesis because the prompt is asking for you to speak personally about someone in your life, but we still avoided phrases like *I will tell you* or *This essay is about*.

On the next page, you will see a flow chart to help you construct a thesis statement. It will help you ensure that it is clear, debatable, organized, and grammatically correct.

Reading Comprehension Questions

1. What is the purpose of a thesis statement?

2. Describe the elements that make a strong thesis.

3. What problems often weaken a thesis?

ACTIVITY

Writing the Thesis Statement / Flowchart

Use the flowchart below to draft and revise a thesis statement for the following prompt to meet all the requirements. You should use this flow chart when first and second person point-of-view is prohibited.

Prompt: *What are the characteristics and habits of a successful student?*

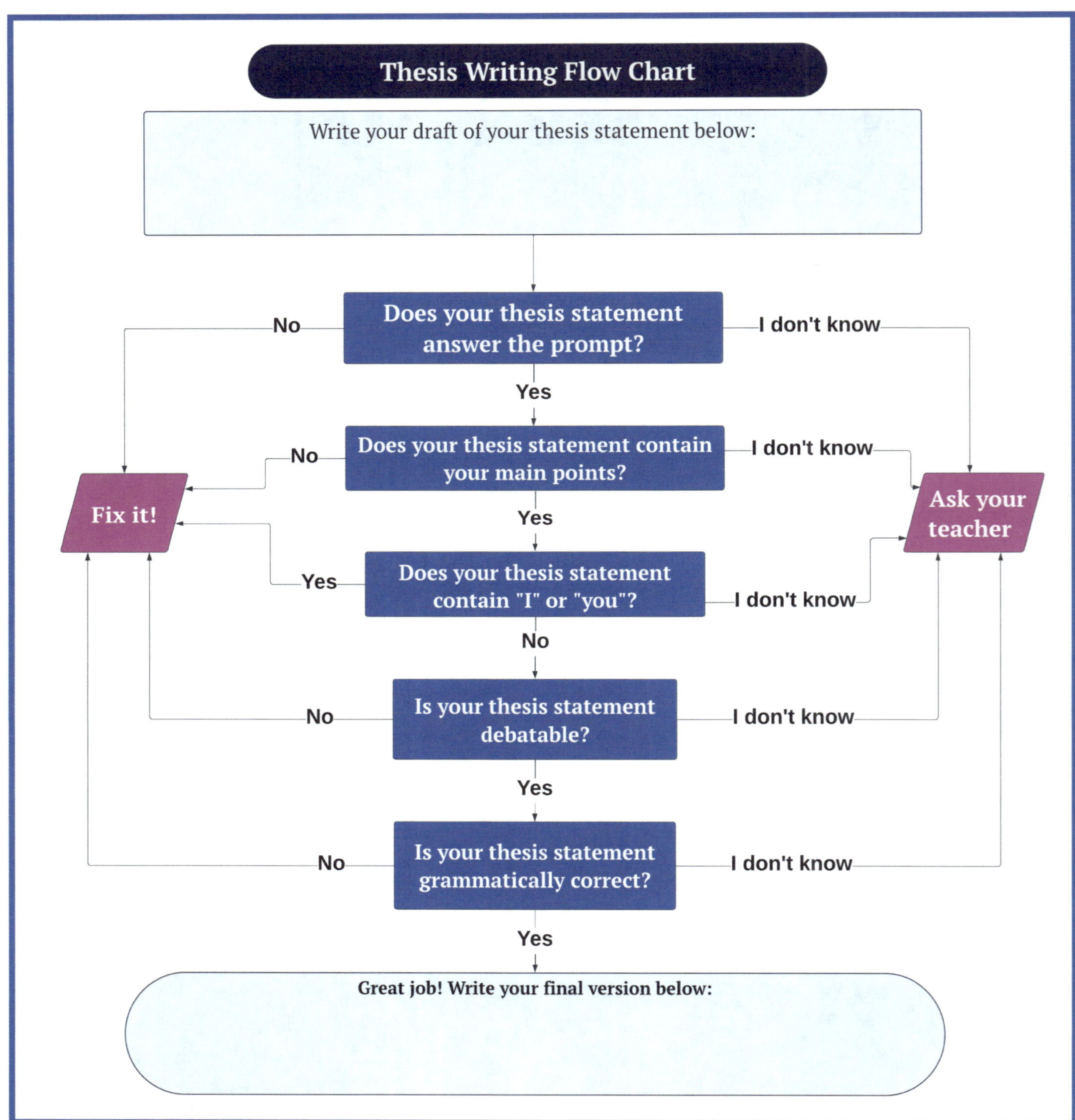

ACTIVITY

Writing the Thesis Statement / Flowchart

Use the flowchart below to draft and revise a thesis statement for the following prompt to meet all the requirements. You should use this flow chart when first and second person point-of-view is permitted.

Prompt: *What is your favorite time of year? Provide two to three main reasons to support your opinion.*

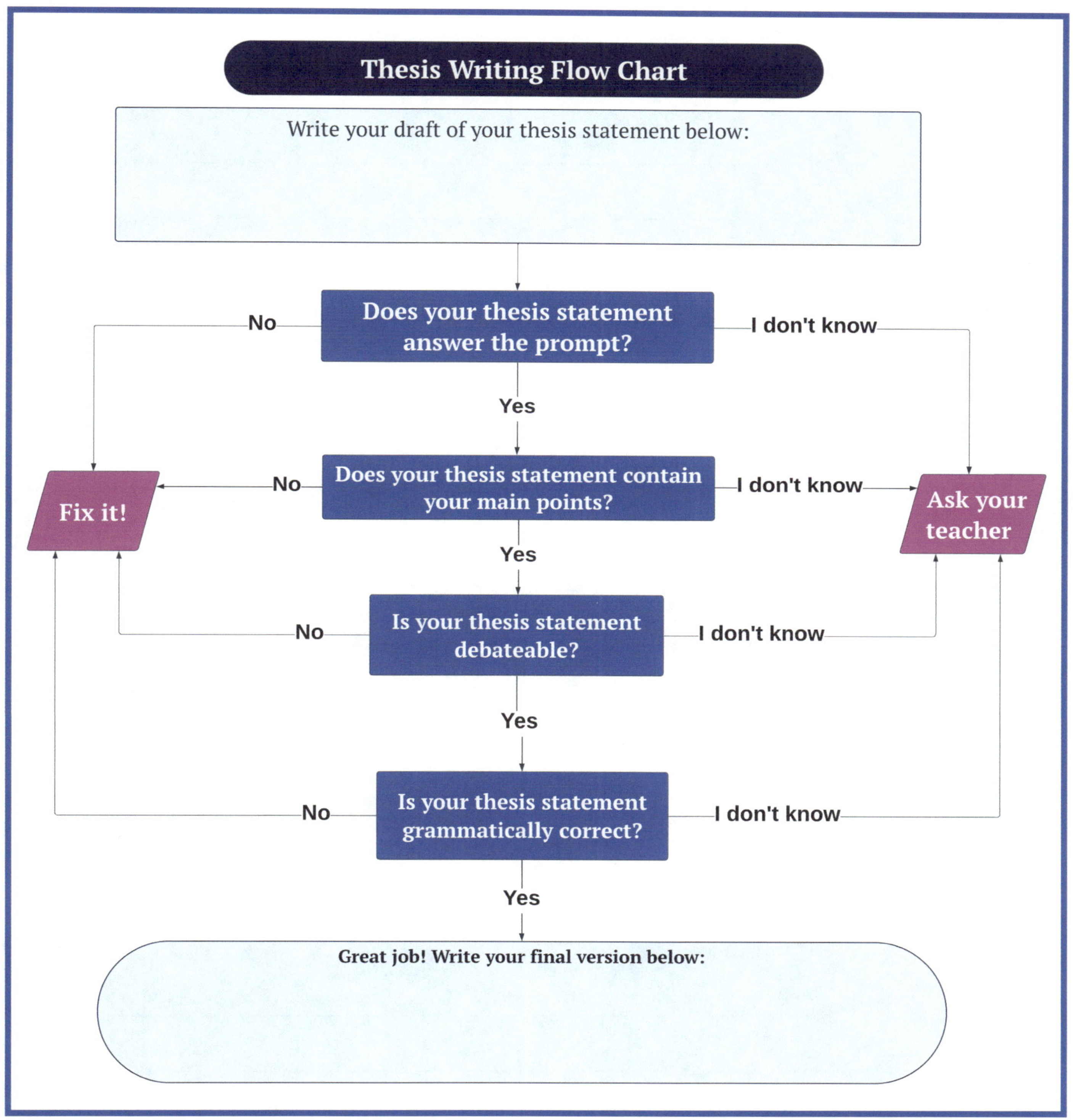

ACTIVITY

Identifying Thesis Statements / Practice

For each sentence below, identify whether or not it is a strong thesis. For those that are strong claims, explain why they are strong. For those that are not strong, correct them so that they are. You may need to add more information to correct them.

1. I am going to tell you why the platypus is amazing with its unique body shape and capabilities.

Strong **Weak**

Explanation/Correction: ______________________________

____

2. Piano serves as the best first instrument because of its versatility and availability.

Strong **Weak**

Explanation/Correction: ______________________________

____

3. Schools should not assign homework because it does not significantly increase test scores, it causes unneeded stress, and it inhibits beneficial extracurricular activities.

Strong **Weak**

Explanation/Correction: ______________________________

____

4. Many people differ on whether the benefits of standardized testing outweigh the harms.

Strong **Weak**

Explanation/Correction: ______________________________

____

ACTIVITY

Identifying Thesis Statements / Practice

For each sentence below, identify whether or not it is a strong thesis. For those that are strong claims, explain why they are strong. For those that are not strong, correct them so that they are. You may need to add more information to correct them.

5. The benefits of daily participation in competitive sports should be weighed against potential harms.

Strong **Weak**

Explanation/Correction: ____

____

6. Students should have nightly homework because it provides extra practice, prepares students for adulthood, and encourages self-reliance.

Strong **Weak**

Explanation/Correction: ____

____

7. This essay is about the various reasons why students should not have standardized tests such as the stress it causes and the excessive time it takes.

Strong **Weak**

Explanation/Correction: ____

____

8. Integrity is an important issue to discuss.

Strong **Weak**

Explanation/Correction: ____

____

ACTIVITY

Writing Thesis Statements / Practice

Create a strong thesis statement for each prompt below. Refer back to your brainstorming webs from chapter 1. If you did not create a brainstorming map for the thesis listed, you may need to first jot down your ideas before crafting a thesis.

1. **Prompt:** Think about a person you admire. Why do you admire them? Explain in a five-paragraph essay.

Strong thesis: ____

____

2. **Prompt:** Which season is your favorite? Explain why this season is your favorite in a four-paragraph essay.

Strong thesis: ____

____

3. **Prompt:** Write an essay about the importance of hard work.

Strong thesis: ____

____

4. **Prompt:** What are the characteristics and habits of a successful student? Explain in a four- to five-paragraph essay.

Strong thesis: ____

____

5. **Prompt:** Think about your favorite book. Write an essay providing three strong reasons why everyone should read it.

Strong thesis: ____

____

ACTIVITY

Writing Thesis Statements / Practice

Create a strong thesis statement for each prompt below. Refer back to your brainstorming webs from chapter 1. If you did not create a brainstorming map for the thesis listed, you may need to first jot down your ideas before crafting a thesis.

6. **Prompt:** What are the benefits of learning a foreign language? Explain in a four- to five-paragraph essay.

Strong thesis: ______________________________

____

7. **Prompt:** What are the benefits of participating in a study abroad program? Explain in a four- to five-paragraph essay.

Strong thesis: ______________________________

____

8. **Prompt:** Write an essay about what makes you unique. Write about at least two different characteristics.

Strong thesis: ______________________________

____

9. **Prompt:** What are some of the harms of excessive screen time or use of social media by students?

Strong thesis: ______________________________

____

10. **Prompt:** Choose a career that you may want to pursue. What makes you interested in this career?

Strong thesis: ______________________________

____

ESSAY

Creative Writing / Practice Makes Perfect

Spend some time writing on the following if/then question. You can answer the question by showing it in a fictional story or by writing it as a traditional essay. First, brainstorm your ideas in the space below and use it to form your thesis statement (even a creative story can have one sentence that captures the main idea). Then, answer the prompt on the next page. First person is permitted.

If you could travel anywhere in the world, where would you go and why? What would you want to see and experience there?

Brainstorming Space:

Thesis:

ESSAY

Creative Writing / Practice Makes Perfect

Now that you have brainstormed your ideas and formed your thesis statement, answer the prompt below in complete sentences. When you are done, go back and reread your work and revise for typos and grammar errors, and with your teacher's permission, share it with a classmate.

If you could travel anywhere in the world, where would you go and why? What would you want to see and experience there?

ESSAY

LE MARAIS

Your essay map or outline provides the structure you need before you begin to write your paragraphs. Once you have the framework organized, you can begin construction. Just like a builder would not begin without a blueprint, neither should you begin without an outline.

Art by Frank Boston

CHAPTER

Essay Maps

ROADMAP

- Identify ways to add supporting details to your main points.
- Learn how to craft an essay map.
- Practice creating essay maps for various prompts.

THALES OUTCOME
Nº 3

A person with **Self-Reliance** *shows confidence to depend on one's own powers and resources to meet all of one's needs.*

The next stage of writing the essay is to craft an essay map or outline. There are many correct ways to structure an outline which means you will need to rely on your own thoughts and ideas to create strong main points with organized, detailed evidence.

Essay Maps & Adding Detail

Now that you have your roadmap (i.e. your thesis) prepared, it is time to add more detailed directions to lead your reader to your destination. Before you begin writing the essay's paragraphs, you must further develop and organize your main points into an **essay map** or outline. In this chapter, we will be discussing a basic main point essay map, and we will learn about crafting detailed outlines in Chapter 13. An essay map, as you see below, gives you a chance to write out your thesis, main points, and supporting details. First, write your strong thesis statement at the top of your map. If you had a detailed brainstorming map, filling in the main points and supporting details should be fairly easy. Except for the thesis, the map should contain key words and phrases only, not complete sentences, just as you did in your brainstorming map. You will have plenty of time to craft strong sentences very soon.

The essay map below gives space for three main points; however, every essay, like every author, is unique. Your teacher may give you a set number of main points for your essay or it may be flexible. Not every essay has to have exactly three main points. If you are unsure of the requirements on a particular assignment, check your directions or speak with your teacher.

Let us return to our thesis from the previous chapter and use it to form an essay map. You may recall one thesis we formed: ***I admire my father because he is kind to everyone and supportive of all my endeavors.*** On the essay map, we first write this sentence in the

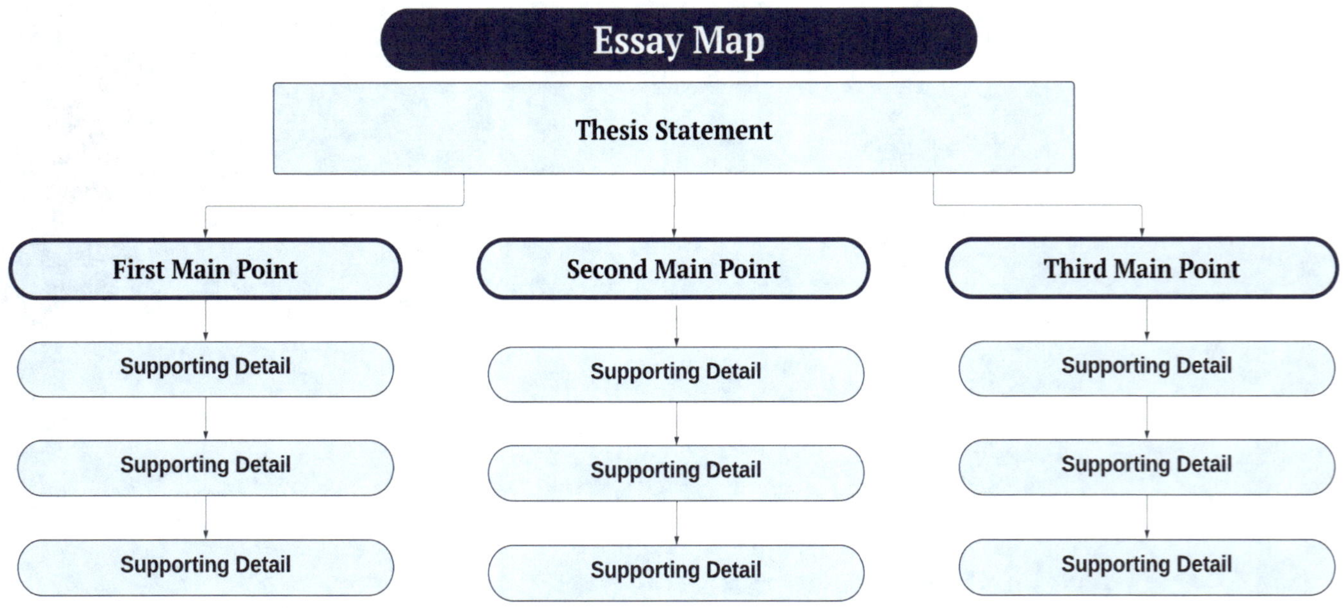

Vocabulary

Essay Map
A visual way to chart out the main points and their corresponding support points before writing an essay.

Evidence
Information that supports the claim. It could include facts, statistics, personal experience, etc.

Thesis Statement rectangle. Then, in the *First Main Point* and *Second Main Point* sections, we write those two main reasons that we chose, that he is *kind* and *supportive.* Beneath each of those main reasons, we add details that prove our main points and how they support our thesis. These details are your **evidence** — your facts, reasoning, or other information that proves your claim true. When trying to determine strong supporting details, think about your question words, primarily *how* or *why*. Information that answers *why* will provide you with more reasons, and information that answers *how* will provide you with more support. We primarily asked *why* questions when devising the main points for our thesis, but now we will focus more on answering the question *how* in order to explain and prove our main points.

So, *how* is this father kind? He shows his kindness by going out of his way to help at the scene of a car accident, by spending his free time volunteering at an animal shelter, and by helping his elderly neighbor with her grocery shopping and other errands. And *how* is this father supportive? He supports his child when she struggles on her homework and goes out of his way to encourage and support her theatrical pursuits.

We will discuss presenting and analyzing evidence in more detail in our chapter on body paragraphs. For now, just focus on providing proof in your supporting details to show or explain how that main point is true. Your essay map will look something like this:

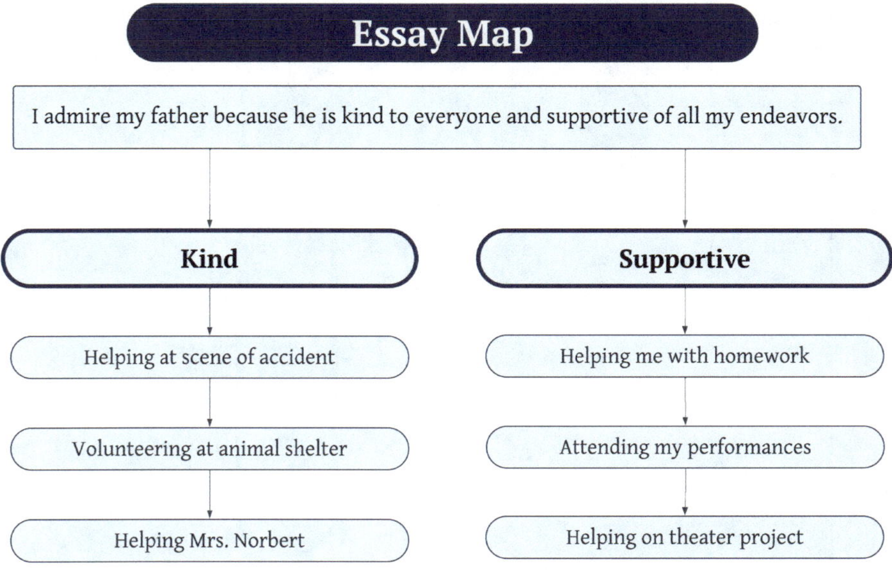

ACTIVITY

Creating Your Essay Map / Practice

Use a thesis you created on page 44 or 45 to fill in the following essay map.

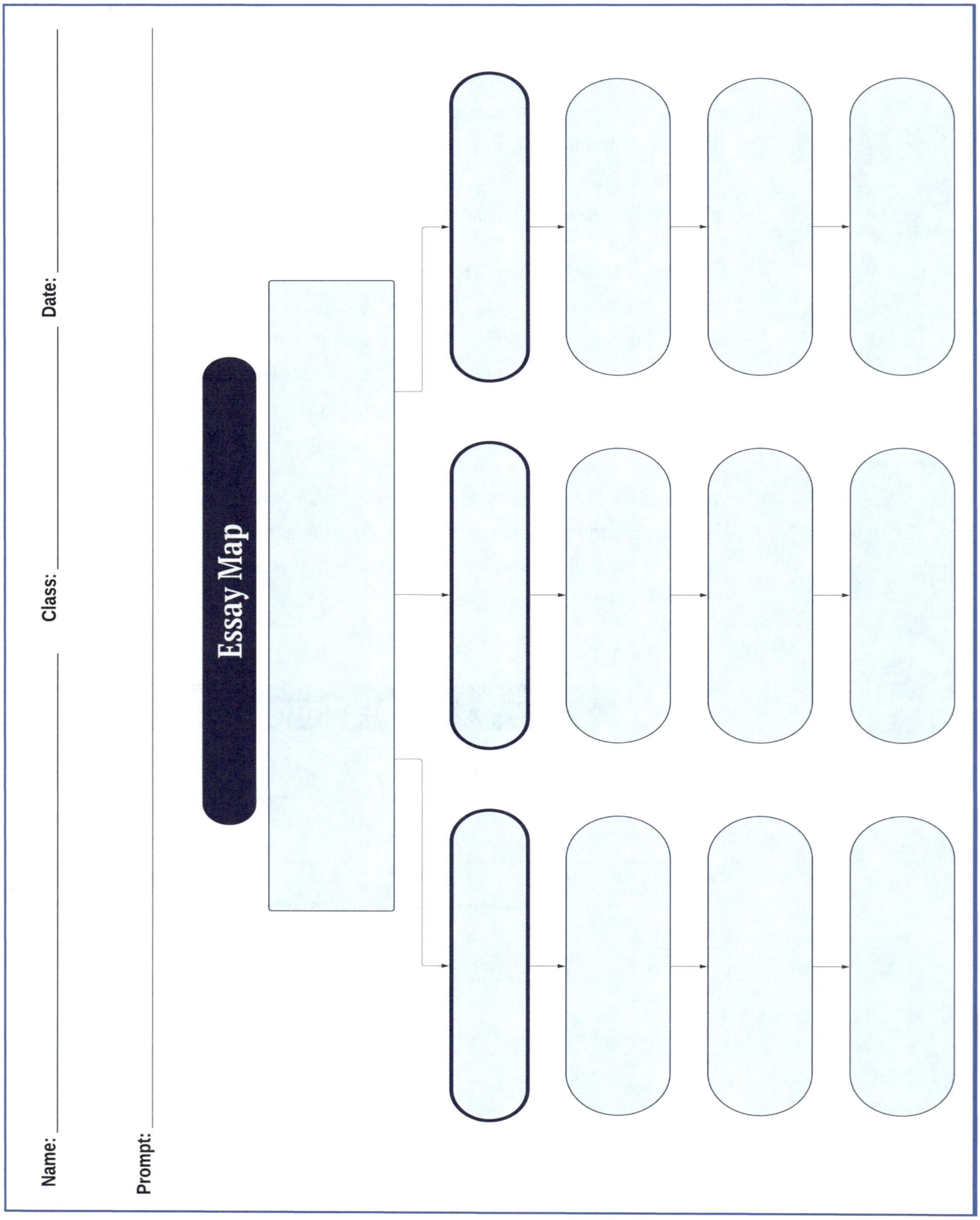

Name: ______ Class: ______ Date: ______

Prompt: ______

Essay Map

ACTIVITY

Creating Your Essay Map / Practice

Use a thesis you created on page 44 or 45 to fill in the following essay map.

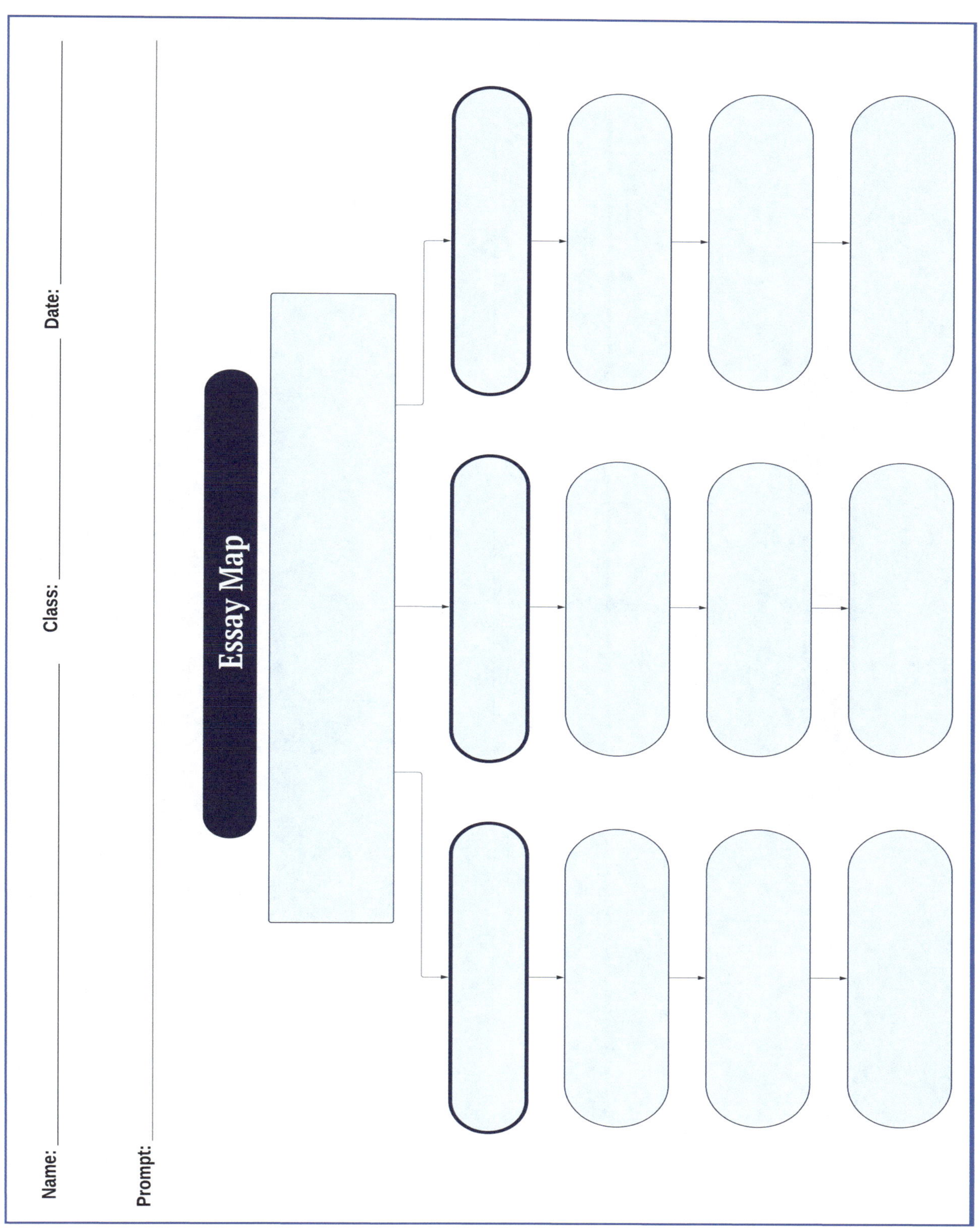

ACTIVITY

Creating Your Essay Map / Practice

Use a thesis you created on page 44 or 45 to fill in the following essay map.

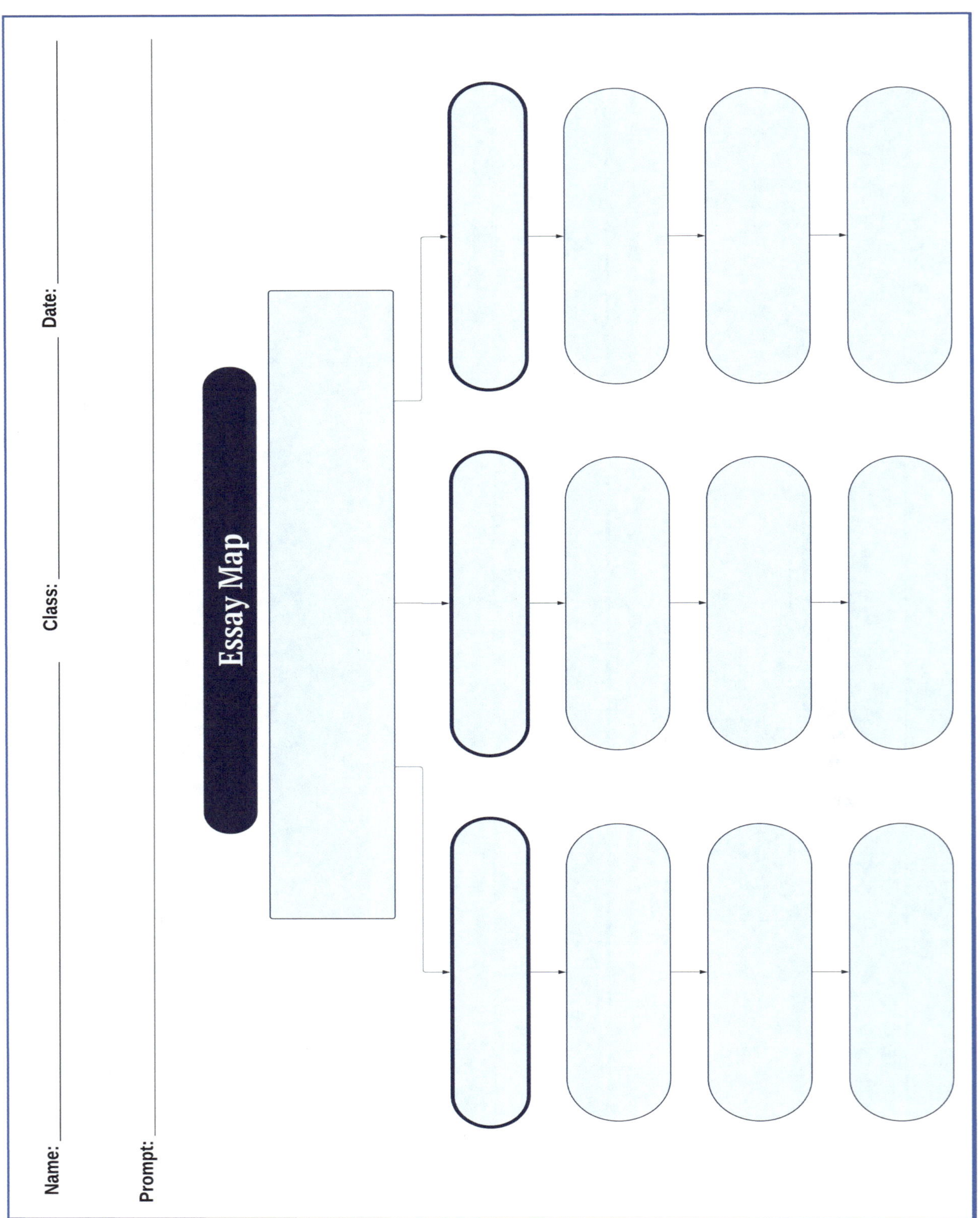

ESSAY

Journal Writing / Practice Makes Perfect

Remember, the more you write, the better you'll get. Before you begin on the following prompt, use the space below to brainstorm your ideas and come up with a thesis, but do not worry about filling out an essay map. On the next page, answer the prompt. When you are done, go back and reread your work and revise for typos and grammar errors, and with your teacher's permission, share it with a classmate. First person is permitted.

What is something you're really good at? Describe it and how you developed this skill/talent.

Brainstorming Space:

Thesis:

ESSAY

Journal Writing / Practice Makes Perfect

Now the you have jotted down your ideas, answer the prompt in complete sentences. When you are done, go back and reread your work and revise for typos and grammar errors, and with your teacher's permission, share it with a classmate.

What is something you're really good at? Describe it and how you developed this skill/talent.

MOUNTAINS, WATERCOLOR LANDSCAPE

Artwork by Hanna

Section II
Paragraphs

CHAPTERS

MOUNTAIN LANDSCAPE

The introduction to your essay provides the big picture of your essay, much like this watercolor gives a broad view of the surrounding landscape.

Painting by Мария Тарасова

CHAPTER

The Introduction

ROADMAP

- Understand the various elements of a strong introductory paragraph.
- Distinguish between different types of hooks.
- Practice writing quality hooks and introductions.

THALES OUTCOME

№ 13

A person with **Well-developed People & Communication Skills** *can effectively share a clear message.*

The first paragraph of an essay is the introduction. This first impression your reader gets of your writing is your chance to grab your reader's interest and help them engage with your claim. The introduction must be clear, interesting, and organized in order to provide a strong foundation for the rest of your essay.

The Introduction Paragraph

NOW THAT WE HAVE a roadmap and directions, it is finally time to begin crafting our paragraphs. A **paragraph** is a group of sentences with one central theme. For your writing to be organized, it is important that each paragraph only discusses one point. If you have a second point to make, you will generally start a new paragraph. An essay always begins with an introductory paragraph followed by a varying number of body paragraphs and ends with the conclusion. In this chapter, we will discuss the introductory paragraph.

The **introduction**, or introductory paragraph, is always the first paragraph of an essay and provides an overview of what your essay is about. It should begin with a **hook** — a catchy opener that makes the reader interested in your essay and encourages them to continue reading. The introductory paragraph also contains the **thesis statement**, usually as the very last sentence. In between the hook and the thesis statement, your introduction may also contain background information or a rebuttal of common counter-arguments, depending on the topic of the essay. Let us start by delving more deeply into hooks, the very first sentence of your essay.

Your goal with the very first sentence of your essay is to grab the attention of your reader, making them want to keep reading. If your first sentences are boring, vague, or **cliché**, your reader will not be as engaged and interested in reading the rest of your argument. This catchy opener is known as your hook. Like a hook on a fishing line, your hook should catch your reader and reel them in to the rest of your essay. Paired with the **clincher**, which we will discuss in a subsequent chapter on conclusions, the hook serves as the first of a pair of bookends that surround your essay.

Types of Hooks

There are many different ways to hook your reader at the start of your essay, but we will discuss a few categories and some examples to get you started. Certain types of hooks lend themselves more toward certain essay types, while others are tricky because they initially sound easy but are tough to make unique.

An Announcement or Challenging Statement

An announcement or statement gets straight to the point. It engages the reader with a short, powerful idea that will be developed throughout the essay. When you use this type of hook, make sure to choose strong, active verbs to create a more powerful sentence. It is

The introduction is the first paragraph of an essay and is responsible for grabbing your reader's interest, providing any necessary context, and laying out your essay's main points.

Vocabulary

Paragraph
A group of sentences with one central theme.

Introduction
The first paragraph of an essay that grabs the reader's attention and presents what the essay is about. It begins with the hook and ends with the thesis.

Hook
A catchy opener that makes your audience interested in your essay and encourages them to continue reading.

Thesis statement
One to two sentences that present the claim that you plan to argue for in your essay. It should clearly identify the topic, your point of view, and the main ways you plan to prove or explain that point of view.

Cliché
A phrase or expression that is so overused that it is no longer interesting.

okay if this statement is controversial. You can use the next few sentences to back up or explain this statement.

Examples:

Nobody enjoys homework.
This sentence would be relevant to a persuasive essay arguing why students should have less homework.

The beauty of Cannon Beach in Oregon surpasses every other beach in the world.
This sentence would be relevant to a narrative essay about a favorite vacation or perhaps a persuasive essay on why northwestern, rocky beaches are superior to the traditional white, sandy beaches of the East Coast.

A Fact or Statistic

A fact or statistic can be a great way to get your reader interested in your research paper. Make sure that you choose a statistic that is relevant to your particular essay. You may even use the same statistic in one of your body paragraphs later on to support one of your main points.

Examples:

According to the Better Sleep Council, teenagers in the United States spend more than 2 hours on homework every night.
This statistic would be a great start to an essay about how students' homework load should be decreased.

According to the CDC, only 24% of school age children participate in 60 minutes of physical activity each day.
This fact would be a strong hook for an essay about how students should have less homework because it decreases students' physical activity time. It could also be a hook for an essay about requiring P.E. in school or extending recess.

A Question

Questions can make interesting hooks if you take the time to craft one carefully. Make sure it is unique, interesting, and thought-provoking. It should generally not be written in second person (using the word "you"). For example, do not say *Do you like homework?* or *Did you know...?* (If you are tempted by this second one, try stating an interesting fact instead of asking your reader if they knew that fact). These types of questions are too broad, overused, and do not add anything to your writing. Additionally, remember that just because you used a question as your first sentence does not mean you have crafted a quality hook. Choose a question that is intriguing and that is answered by your essay.

Examples:

What is the difference between a job and a career?
This question would be a great start to a personal essay about what career you are interested in, but you would want to be sure to answer this question in the process.

What sets apart the successful middle-school student?
This question would be a strong way to begin an expository essay discussing middle school study skills.

An Anecdote

An anecdote is like a very short story. Remember, a hook's job is just to grab the attention of the reader, so if you choose to use an anecdote as the start of your essay, be sure to limit it to just a couple captivating sentences. It can be a hypothetical story, a story from your own life, or a real story you found through research.

Example:

After two minutes of administering CPR, a wave of relief washed over the paramedic as he saw the boy begin to breathe, and he was reminded why he chose this career.
This short story would be a unique way to begin an essay about how rewarding a job in medicine can be or an essay arguing that paramedics are under-appreciated.

A Quotation

Quotations can be an effective way to begin an essay, but be careful, they can become cliché and lose their effectiveness. That said, a quotation can be a very useful way to begin a literary analysis essay. By beginning with a quotation from the novel, you have accomplished two things: you have given us an interesting start to the essay and indicated which book you will be analyzing.

Vocabulary

Anecdote
A very brief story that is interesting or amusing in some way.

Metaphor
A figure of speech where one thing is stated to be another different thing without using *like* or *as*.

Simile
A figure of speech using *like* or *as* to compare two seemingly unrelated things.

Background information
Information that the reader needs in order to understand the general topic of the essay more clearly.

Counterargument
An argument that goes against the main claim of the essay.

Rebuttal
A response disproving or weakening the reasons against the main claim of the essay.

You can also use a quotation from other sources or famous people, but be sure that it is relevant to your particular essay and says something unique and catchy, not just a really famous sentence generally related to your topic. For instance, you should only use the famous quotation from Gandhi who said, "You must be the change you wish to see in the world" if your essay is about a change that needs to be made to make the world a better place, one that an ordinary person could accomplish. If your essay is about bullying in social media, but not about what the average person can do to mitigate this issue or help in some way, then no matter how famous the above quotation is, it would be irrelevant. Anytime you use a quotation in your writing, be sure that you introduce the quotation by saying who said it or other contextual information.

Examples:

Ernest Hemingway once said, "Writing is rewriting."
This quotation would be relevant to an essay about various methods for revising an essay, but if it were about why you want to be an author, it would not fit.

Football coach Vince Lombardi famously said, "If you can't accept losing, you can't win."
This quotation would be relevant to an essay about good sportsmanship, but if your essay is merely about your favorite sport, or football in general, it would not serve as an adequate hook for your topic.

A Metaphor or Simile

A **metaphor** or **simile** (pronounced *si-muh-lee*) is a figure of speech that can be used anywhere in your writing, especially in creative writing, and is another effective way to grab your reader's attention. A simile uses the word *like* or *as* to compare two seemingly unrelated things, such as *The participant in the hot-dog-eating contest gobbled the food down like a pig*. A metaphor is similar, but it does not use the word "like" or "as." An example would be *My dog is a pig when he eats*. We understand that the dog does not actually transform into a pig when he eats, rather we are using the word metaphorically to show how messily or excessively he eats.

Examples:

The summer sun is like a familiar friend, always bringing me joy and comfort after the dark days of winter and the rainy days of spring.
This hook contains a simile and would be a good starting point for an essay about how summer is your favorite season.

Homework is a storm cloud over many students' lives, casting a shadow over all they do.
This hook contains a metaphor and could introduce an essay about the drawbacks of homework or why it should be reduced. The essay would proceed to show how homework is like a storm cloud.

Connecting the Hook and Thesis

After you have written your hook, there are a couple different options on what to write next. If your hook is already a few sentences long and directly and easily connects to your thesis, you may just go ahead and finish your introductory paragraph by writing your thesis sentence. Remember, the thesis should almost

Introduction Example

Sirens wailed in my driveway. I watched in shock as the paramedics rushed into our house and over to my brother, who lay unmoving on the floor. After two minutes of administering CPR, a wave of relief washed over me as I heard my

brother cough and saw his chest rise and fall as he took a few shallow breaths. When I am older, I plan to volunteer as a paramedic in order to help save lives and make a difference in my community.

always be the last sentence of your introduction. Here is an example of a complete introduction paragraph composed of just a hook and a thesis:

Although this introduction gets its point across with only a hook and thesis, most of the time, you will need additional sentences to connect the hook to the thesis. Even in the above example, the introduction would be strengthened by an additional sentence between the hook and the thesis such as, *That moment is when I knew what I wanted to do.* You may have noticed that we underlined the thesis above. The sentences that were not underlined were the hook sentences. Adding this extra transition sentence after the hook sentences (our anecdote) but before the thesis would have strengthened that connection and provided a more smooth transition, leading to an even stronger introduction.

Other Introductory Elements

Besides the hook and the thesis, there are a couple of other elements that may be needed to strengthen your introduction. The first is **background information**. This term refers to information such as historical context or definitions that the reader needs in order to understand your general topic more clearly. For example, if you are writing a paper about Martin Luther King Jr.'s effect on the Civil Rights movement, generally knowing King's background as a minister and activist in the 1960s would help readers understand the context of what they are reading. The following is a sample introduction that contains background information:

Introduction Example

Martin Luther King, Jr. once said, "Our lives begin to end the day we become silent about things that matter." King was not silent. He began his career as a Baptist minister but was most famous for his role as the leader of the civil rights movement. King's nonviolent campaigns, including the Montgomery Bus Boycott and the March on Washington, helped bring the nation closer to freedom and equality for all citizens.

Can you find the hook, background information, and thesis sentence? Let's break down that paragraph into its different elements.

First, we have the hook (a quotation): Martin Luther King, Jr. once said, "Our lives begin to end the day we become silent about things that matter."

Then, we have a transitional sentence: King was not silent. This sentence connects the quotation about being "silent on things that matter" to the rest of the introduction and the thesis statement about making an important change in the world.

Third, we have some very basic background information about who Martin Luther King, Jr. was: He began his career as a Baptist minister but was most famous for his role as the leader of the civil rights movement. Notice that we only included one simple, relevant fact. We are not saying when or where he born, whom he married, or the names of his children. If you are including background information, you need to determine what facts are important for the reader to know in order to understand what comes next.

Finally, we have our thesis statement: King's nonviolent campaigns, including the Montgomery Bus Boycott and the March on Washington, helped bring the nation closer to freedom and equality for all citizens.

From this thesis we can tell that this essay will focus on two main events: the Montgomery Bus Boycott and the March on Washington. Then the author will show how these two events helped bring the United States closer to establishing equal freedoms and rights for all people.

Another element that can be found in some introductions is the **counter-argument**. Often found in persuasive essays, the counter-argument presents an idea against the main claim of the thesis. Including a brief reference to opposing ideas shows that the author has considered both sides, then and gives the author a chance to disprove the argument in the form of a **rebuttal**, a more advanced element that will be discussed further in the chapter on persuasive writing.

All in all, your introduction serves to pull the reader in and briefly show the reader what you will be proving. An introduction with a catchy hook that flows smoothly into your thesis gives a good first impression of your ideas and helps the reader follow your reasoning more easily.

Reading Comprehension Questions

1. What is the purpose of a hook?

2. Describe the elements of an introduction and how they work together.

3. Where should the thesis statement be located?

ACTIVITY

Writing Hooks / Practice

Create a strong hook of the indicated type for each thesis below. Because the thesis has been provided for you, you may need write a hypothetical hook. For example, you can make a fictional anecdote about the compassionate grandmother if you don't have a real life experience to use.

1. **Thesis:** The person I admire most is my grandmother, whose compassion and unwavering love have shaped not only my life but also the lives of those around her.

Metaphor or simile: ______________________________

____

Anecdote: ______________________________

____

2. **Thesis:** My favorite season is fall because the air is cool and crisp air, the foliage is beautiful, and the holidays are some of my favorites.

Announcement or challenging statement: ______________________________

____

Question: ______________________________

____

3. **Thesis:** Learning a foreign language offers a multitude of benefits, including expanding one's mental capacity, improving one's understanding of other cultures, and increasing one's career opportunities.

Fact or Statistic: ______________________________

____

Quotation: ______________________________

____

ACTIVITY

Writing Hooks / Practice

Create a strong hook of the indicated type for each thesis below. Because the thesis has been provided for you, you may need write a hypothetical hook. For example, you can make a fictional anecdote about the compassionate grandmother if you don't have a real life experience to use.

4. **Thesis:** All students should participate in a study abroad program because it fosters independence, improves their career prospects, and allows them to experience different ways of life .

Fact or Statistic: ____

____

Question: ____

____

5. **Thesis:** Pizza stands out as the best food because of its versatility and ability to satisfy a wide range of taste preferences.

Metaphor or simile: ____

____

Announcement or challenging statement: ____

____

6. **Thesis:** I plan to pursue a career in teaching because it is rewarding and offers the opportunity to inspire future generations.

Anecdote:____

____

Quotation: ____

____

ESSAY

Creative Writing / Practice Makes Perfect

Remember, the more you write, the better you'll get. Let's have some fun writing on the following if/then question. You can answer the question by showing it in a fictional story or by writing it as a traditional essay. Try to give your story/essay a catchy opener (hook). When you are done, go back and reread your work and revise for typos and grammatical errors, and with your teacher's permission, share it with a classmate.

If you could have any superpower, what would it be and how would you use it to make a positive impact on the world?

ROME AT SUNSET

This image beautifully represents the city of Rome at sunset. Constructing your body paragraphs is a lot like constructing the building of a great city.

Image by Stockbym

CHAPTER

Body Paragraphs

ROADMAP

- Learn the key elements of strong body paragraphs.
- Identify the parts of a body paragraph.
- Practice constructing body paragraphs.

THALES OUTCOME

Nº 1

A person with **Unfailing Integrity** *follows a strong code of ethics with honesty in all situations.*

The body paragraphs of your essay are where you present your evidence. It is essential that your work is authentic and that you present your evidence honestly, without any attempt to mislead your audience or misrepresent your information in any way.

Writing Body Paragraphs

NOW THAT WE HAVE a roadmap and directions, it is finally time to craft the main body of our essay. As we discussed earlier, a **paragraph** is a group of sentences with one central theme. For your writing to be organized, it is important that each paragraph only discusses one point. If you have a second point to make, you will generally start a new paragraph. Remember, essays usually have three main types of paragraphs: introduction paragraphs, body paragraphs, and conclusion paragraphs. Now, we will proceed to body paragraphs.

A **body paragraph** is a paragraph that presents one main point to prove the thesis of your essay. You can have any number of body paragraphs in an essay, but the most common number is three (the number of body paragraphs in what is known as the standard five-paragraph essay). Body paragraphs begin with a **topic sentence** that summarizes the main point and presents the **claim** of that paragraph. A strong topic sentence does not merely report the fact that you will be making a point but gives the actual claim you are making. For example, if you were writing an essay on the benefits of playing soccer, *My next point is about teamwork* would not make an adequate topic sentence. Instead, you would want to say something such as, *Soccer also helps players learn teamwork.* This statement is debatable and references back to your overall thesis about the benefits of playing soccer, which your subsequent sentences will prove true.

You may be thinking that a sentence like *Soccer helps players learn teamwork* sounds a lot like a thesis statement itself, and you'd be right! The topic sentence or claim is basically a thesis with only one main point — the one you will be discussing in this paragraph.

Although there is nothing wrong with calling this sentence the "topic sentence," we will often use the phrase "claim" to emphasize that these sentences should do more than just present the topic that the paragraph is about and to encourage you to write strong sentences.

In addition to an clear claim, a strong body paragraph must contain good quality **evidence**. Evidence follows the topic sentence and proves the claim you made in that topic sentence. If your claim sentence stated *Soccer also helps players learn teamwork*, then each subsequent sentence would prove *how* soccer helps players learn teamwork. You can support your claim with facts or statistics, logical reasoning, or personal experience. The more specific and detailed your evidence, the stronger your paragraph. Remember, there

Body paragraphs make up the majority of your essay. Each body paragraph presents one reason in support of your thesis, evidence to support that reason, and analysis of that evidence.

Vocabulary

Paragraph
A group of sentences with one central theme.

Body Paragraph
A paragraph that presents one main point to prove the thesis of your essay

Topic Sentence
Also known as a claim, this sentence is the first sentence of a body paragraph that provides the main point that you will be arguing for in the paragraph.

Claim
A main point from your thesis that you are arguing for in a particular paragraph.

Evidence
Information that supports your claim. It could include facts, statistics, personal experience, etc.

Analysis
An explanation of the evidence and how it supports the claim.

Wrap-up
The last sentence in a body paragraph that gives a sense of closure to the paragraph. It may also provide a transition into the next main point.

should only be one main point in each body paragraph, so each sentence in your body paragraph should directly support the claim sentence of that paragraph. Just because one sentence is relevant to another, does not mean both were relevant to the claim of the paragraph. We will discuss this concept further in our chapter on organization.

After presenting your evidence, it is important that you analyze or explain it, especially if your proof is a quote from a source. Simply providing a quotation (the evidence) usually does not adequately prove your claim or show its significance. Your **analysis** goes into detail regarding how that particular evidence proves the claim that began your paragraph. Be careful of the word ***this***. Often, students are tempted to follow their evidence with the phrase ***This is why*** or ***This shows***, but these are very vague and simplistic ways to analyze your evidence. Instead, used specific nouns in place of the pronoun "this" and active verbs instead of the "to be" verb.

Weak Analysis	***Strong Analysis***
The study found that submitted resumes that included study abroad experience were 20% more likely to receive a callback for an interview than those that did not (Cheng and Florick). This shows that studying abroad improves students' chance to get an interview.	*The study found that resumes that included study abroad experience were 20% more likely to receive a callback for an interview than those that did not (Cheng and Florick). Because employers recognize the skills gained from studying abroad, students will boost their employability by pursing these types of educational opportunities.*

Notice how the weak example uses the phrase ***this shows*** and primarily restates what the study found. The strong analysis example delves deeper into what the study found, providing an explanation of why studying abroad improves students' career opportunities. The analysis portion of your paragraph is especially important in research essays, so we will return to this idea in our chapter about incorporating research.

It is important to note that you often have more than one piece of evidence in a single body paragraph. Each time you have evidence, you should provide an analysis of that evidence. For this reason, the evidence-analysis part of your body paragraph may repeat multiple times, but only have one claim and wrap-up.

The **wrap-up**, a concluding sentence that wraps up your idea, ends your body paragraph. It often contains key words from your claim, but should not be exactly the same as the sentence that began the paragraph. Again, be careful of phrases like *This is why* or *This shows*. These are vague and do not add any value to your paragraph. For example, returning to our claim *Soccer also helps players learn teamwork,* it would not be an acceptable wrap-up to simply say, *This is why soccer helps players learn teamwork*. Instead, you could say something like *By participating in soccer, students improve their teamwork, a skill essential for success.*

The wrap-up sentence may also provide a transition into the next paragraph if it leads into another one of your points. However, this technique is more advanced and it is difficult to do smoothly, so you will want to wait to try this technique until you are proficient at basic essay writing. In the following chart, the first strong example shows a basic wrap-up, while the second also provides a transition into the next point.

Weak Wrap-up	Strong Wrap-up
This is why students should participate in study abroad programs.	*By participating in study abroad programs, students will learn about other cultures first hand.* *When students learn about other cultures firsthand, they not only gain empathy, they also gain practical life skills.*

You now know all the elements of a basic body paragraph! Let's end our discussion with an example of a body paragraph. Can you identify the purpose of each sentence in this paragraph?

Body Paragraph Example:

One reason students should study abroad is to experience other cultures firsthand. By traveling to a new country, they get to see how people really live with their own eyes. They can learn about their celebrations, food, and beliefs directly. Reading about customs in school is one thing, but living them is a whole different experience. It allows students to be more engaged, remember the concepts more easily, and understand them in the context of the local culture. Overall, studying abroad is essential because it gives students knowledge that cannot be gained in the classroom alone.

As you improve in your writing, it will not always be necessary to write your body paragraphs in this exact order, but you will always include these elements. Altogether, you can use the mnemonic *Captivating Essays Always Win* to help you remember the key elements of a body paragraph: the claim, the evidence, the analysis, and the wrap-up.

You can also feel free to create your own mnemonic to remember these key elements. Perhaps *Curious Elephants Always Wander* or *Clumsy Emus Always Wobble*... whatever helps you remember!

The elements are reviewed at the top of the next page.

Order of Elements in a Body Paragraph:

Claim: *The topic sentence that provides the main idea of the paragraph.*

Evidence: *Research, quotes, and examples to prove your claim.*

Analysis: *An explanation of the evidence that shows how it proves the claim.*

Wrap-up: *A summary or overall take-away from this paragraph and possibly a transition into the next main point.*

Reading Comprehension Questions

1. How is the topic sentence like a thesis statement?

2. What are the four key elements of a body paragraph?

3. Invent another mnemonic for remembering the four parts of a body paragraph.

ACTIVITY

Identifying Strong Claims / Practice

For each statement below, identify whether or not it is a strong claim. For those that are strong claims, explain why they are strong. For those that are not strong, correct them so that they are. You may need to add more information to correct them.

1. I am going to talk about how personal responsibility is an important part of citizenship.

   Claim **Not a Claim**

   Explanation/Correction: ______________________________

   ____

2. Volunteer work is an important issue.

   Claim **Not a Claim**

   Explanation/Correction: ______________________________

   ____

3. One way you can help your country is by exercising personal responsibility.

   Claim **Not a Claim**

   Explanation/Correction: ______________________________

   ____

4. The first reason is teamwork.

   Claim **Not a Claim**

   Explanation/Correction: ______________________________

   ____

ACTIVITY

Identifying Strong Claims / Practice

For each statement below, identify whether or not it is a strong claim. For those that are strong claims, explain why they are strong. For those that are not strong, correct them so that they are. You may need to add more information to correct them.

5. My third point is about developing character.

Claim **Not a Claim**

Explanation/Correction: ______________________________

____

6. One benefit of a year-round education is more time for enriching activities throughout the year.

Claim **Not a Claim**

Explanation/Correction: ______________________________

____

7. I look up to my dad because he is supportive of me.

Claim **Not a Claim**

Explanation/Correction: ______________________________

____

8. Many people say that Vincent Van Gogh is their favorite painter.

Claim **Not a Claim**

Explanation/Correction: ______________________________

____

ACTIVITY

Parts of the Body Paragraph / Practice

For each paragraph below, identify which part of the paragraph is the claim, evidence, analysis, and wrap-up. Be careful of paragraphs that repeat the evidence/analysis portion. These will not necessarily appear consecutively. This assignment could be done individually or as a class discussion, according to the teacher's discretion.

1. If you want a happy, flourishing country, you need virtuous citizens. Every job or position, whether a teacher, businessman, or government official, requires virtues like honesty and justice to do their job well. If most of a country's people are instead dishonest and unjust, the rest of country could not trust them or rely on them. If people do not do their jobs with virtue, their country becomes corrupt and ineffective, the very opposite of a happy and flourishing country.

Claim: ____

Evidence: ____

____

Analysis: ____

____

Wrap-up: ____

2. One benefit of the year-round school calendar is that it improves knowledge retention. Instead of having one long summer break where students forget a lot of information, year-round school splits up the breaks into shorter periods. By keeping the breaks short, the information remains fresh in the students' minds, reducing the need for review. Year-round students tend to do better on tests as well. By avoiding long periods of time off of school, students do not lose as much knowledge. With four shorter breaks rather than one long one, students better retain all the things they learn.

Claim: ____

Evidence: ____

____

Analysis: ____

____

Wrap-up: ____

ACTIVITY

Parts of the Body Paragraph / Practice

For each paragraph below, identify which part of the paragraph is the claim, evidence, analysis, and wrap-up. Be careful of paragraphs that repeat the evidence/analysis portion. These will not necessarily appear consecutively. This assignment could be done individually or as a class discussion, according to the teacher's discretion.

3. Exercise is good for cardiovascular health. When people exercise and get their body moving, their heart beats faster to pump more blood. Because the heart is a muscle, exercise helps it grow stronger just like other muscles. Exercise also helps control blood pressure. Exercises like riding bikes, skating, and running keep the blood flowing well. Heart health is just one of many reasons to exercise regularly.

Claim: ______________________________

Evidence: ______________________________

____

Analysis: ______________________________

____

Wrap-up: ______________________________

4. Dogs make great pets because they provide comfort to their owners. They have an innate ability to provide emotional support through simply being there. Coming home to a dog's wagging tail immediately takes the edge off a stressful day. Many dogs can sense when people are feeling anxious or depressed, and they'll nuzzle up close. Their warm bodies and soft fur are incredibly calming. Dogs also reduce loneliness. They give the owner someone to come home to, take walks with, or simply sit with in silence. By having a dog around, a person will never be without a friend.

Claim: ______________________________

Evidence: ______________________________

____

Analysis: ______________________________

____

Wrap-up: ______________________________

ACTIVITY

Writing Body Paragraphs / Practice

Write a body paragraph for each prompt below. Begin with a claim, followed by evidence and analysis, and end with a wrap-up. Remember to check for spelling and grammar errors when finished.

1. Write a body paragraph on one trait that makes you unique.

2. Write a body paragraph on one study habit that helps students be successful.

ACTIVITY

Writing Body Paragraphs / Practice

Write a body paragraph for each prompt below. Begin with a claim, followed by evidence and analysis, and end with a wrap-up. Remember to check for spelling and grammar errors when finished.

3. Write a body paragraph on one reason to play a team sport in school.

4. Write a body paragraph on one reason why kids should get an allowance.

ESSAY

Journal Writing / Practice Makes Perfect

Remember, the more you write, the better you'll get. Spend some time writing on the following prompt. You can answer the question by showing it in a story or by writing it as a traditional essay. Practice adding good quality evidence, but do not worry about organizing it into set body paragraphs. When you are done, go back and reread your work and revise for typos and grammar errors, and with your teacher's permission, share it with a classmate.

Write about a time when you felt really proud of yourself. What did you accomplish and how did it make you feel?

Essay

WATERCOLOR LANDSCAPE OF SUMMER TUSCANY

Your conclusion provides a send-off and a sense of closure to your essay. Like this beautiful landscape, your conclusion pushes your reader toward some beautiful or important overarching idea.

Painting by Inna Italy

CHAPTER

The Conclusion

ROADMAP

- Learn how to craft strong conclusions.
- Explore different types of clinchers.
- Practice constructing & editing conclusion paragraphs.

THALES OUTCOME

Nº 11

People with* Dreams and Aspirations to Change the World *remember that directed efforts bring them closer to their goals.

The conclusion of your essay ends with a send-off or call to action, a final statement that gives the audience a specific way to implement your ideas or apply them elsewhere in life. This is your chance to make a difference in the world, even in something as small as a conclusion paragraph.

The Conclusion Paragraph

THE FINAL PARAGRAPH of an essay is the **conclusion** paragraph, which sums up the information that you presented in the previous paragraphs. The conclusion should begin with a summary of your thesis and main points, and end with a **clincher** or call-to-action.

The Summary

Your conclusion should begin with a summary. When you present a summary in your conclusion, be sure to actually restate your information. Many students are tempted to use *This is why* or a similar phrase at the beginning of their conclusion. If "this" refers to something in a previous paragraph, then it needs to be restated. "This" is a **pronoun**. A pronoun always pairs with an **antecedent**, the noun that the pronoun refers to. You should not use a pronoun in your essay unless the antecedent of that pronoun appears in the same paragraph. In other words, after providing multiple body paragraphs regarding why you admire your father, you would not then start a new, conclusion paragraph with *This is why I admire my father*. "This" has to point back to a particular antecedent in a recent, prior sentence. The antecedent cannot be the entire body of your essay, which is what you are claiming when you state *This is why* at the start of your conclusion.

So what can you do instead? You first need to present an actual summary of your main points, then you can more appropriately use a pronoun like "this." For example, you could say *My father always helps those in need, not only friends and family, but also strangers. This is why I admire him.* In this example, the main points are first summarized, and "this" refers directly back to the previous sentence.

However, an even better strategy is to completely avoid phrases like *This is why*. Like we talked about in the wrap-up of a body paragraph, phrases like *This is why* are very vague and do not add meaning to your essay. Instead, give the information directly, combining sentences if necessary. We could reword our previous example as, *I admire my father because he always helps those in need, not only friends and family, but also strangers.* Notice how we removed *This is why* by adding *because* and reversing the order of the clauses. The subsequent sentences can then expand upon that sentence to provide a more detailed summary. For example we could follow up with, *He never hesitates to stop at the scene of an accident and always lends a helping hand to our elderly neighbor. He is also an invaluable resource whenever I am preparing for a theater production.* Notice how, in these sentences, we did not just restate the thesis but we actually summarized the main

The conclusion paragraph sums up the information that was presented in the previous paragraphs and ends with a meaningful sentence that brings closure to your essay.

Vocabulary

Conclusion
The last paragraph of an essay that sums up everything that was stated and provides a sense of closure to the essay.

Clincher
The final sentence of the conclusion paragraph that is memorable and provides a send-off to the reader.

Pronoun
A word that takes the place of a noun or noun phrase.

Antecedent
The noun that the pronoun refers to.

Complement
Something that pairs with another in order to enhance them both; i.e. complementary colors.

reasons we used in the body of the essay.

The Clincher

The other element of the conclusion is the clincher. This sentence is the final sentence of your entire essay, and it may be the most difficult sentence of your essay to write. Since it is the last sentence your audience will read, it should provide both a sense of closure and something memorable for your reader.

Bookends

One way to make your clincher especially strong is to think of your hook and clincher as a pair of bookends that holds your essay together. Choosing a hook and clincher that **complement** each other in some way helps you tie your essay altogether. Keep in mind that you must choose both your hook and clincher with this purpose in mind. If you already have a hook, and then you decide later to try to add a complementary clincher, this choice may not work. Not all hooks are compatible with choosing a matching clincher. They are like a matched set and need to be written together. There is nothing wrong with going back and rewriting your hook after finishing the rest of your essay, if you have an idea for a hook and clincher pair. You will often be revising your sentences, and the hook is no exception.

Let us return to one of our hook examples from Chapter 4 to show you how to write a complementary clincher. Our sample question hook was *What is the difference between a job and a career?* Let us expand on this hook and develop it into an introduction with a thesis, so that we can have a better idea of

What is the difference between a job and a career? While a job may simply be a way to pay the bills, a career provides a deeper sense of purpose and fulfillment. This feeling is especially apparent in the field of medicine, with its rigorous demands and challenges. Being a doctor is a rewarding career due to its profound impact on people's lives and the opportunity it brings to serve the local community.

what this hypothetical essay discusses:

We can see from this introduction that the essay will revolve around the rewarding aspects of a career in medicine. When we reach our conclusion, we would first provide a summary of how we proved that being a doctor impacts people's lives and serves the community. Then, we would end that paragraph with a clincher. One way we can end a paragraph is by returning to our question hook: *What is the difference between a job and a career?* We can create a complementary clincher by expanding upon the idea of how being a doctor is not just a job, but a career. Here is a clincher example: *Being a doctor is more than a job to pay the bills, it is a career that inundates your whole life with meaning and purpose.* You can see how we returned to those key words of *job* and *career* from our first sentence, providing a sense of closure to our essay.

So What?

Another way to determine a strong clincher for your essay is to use the "so what?" question. Think of your thesis, and then ask "so what?" "Why should we care?" "Why does that matter?" Let us return to our Martin Luther King Jr. thesis from earlier. In Chapter 4, we said *King's nonviolent campaigns, including the Montgomery Bus Boycott and the March on Washington, helped bring the nation closer to freedom and equality for all citizens.* So what? Why do these things matter? Well, it matters because the civil rights movement was a pivotal time in our history, spurring a fundamental shift in our nation and its laws. Therefore, a clincher that could end this essay may be *These events led by King were instrumental in breaking down the barriers of segregation and injustice, and without them, the nation would not be what it is today.* Don't forget that this sentence would be preceded by a summary of what you said about those events in the body of your essay so that the pronoun "these" has a nearby antecedent.

Broader Implications

You could also choose to ponder the broader implications of your thesis claim in your clincher. Let us again think about our Martin Luther King, Jr. thesis statement. We could put our ideas in the context of modern-day events and say, *King's nonviolent campaigns continue to influence people today as the nation still struggles with what it means to be created equal.* or *While the most dramatic shift in civil rights occurred during this movement that King pioneered, human rights continues to be a major issue today.* By referencing these broader implications in the final sentence of our essay, we leave our readers with something to think about long after they have finished reading our essay. We could also consider how this movement went on to shape human rights in other countries such as India, Northern Ireland, and South Africa. A possible clincher that draws attention to these events would be, *King's powerful campaign transcends time and place, spurring change not only in the United States, but around the world.*

Call to Action

Another type of clincher you can use for your essay is one that provides a "call to action." This provides some sort of actionable goal for your reader. Imagine an essay on the importance of integrity and its affect on the community. A clincher for this essay could be *Every choice matters. By choosing to act with virtue, honesty, and integrity in all situations, everyone can help their community flourish.* Notice how we were even able to make a call to action without writing our sentence in the second person point of view! If you are allowed to use second person, an alternative "call-to-action" clincher for this topic could be *Together, we can make the world a more virtuous place, one right choice at a time* or *Will you make the right choices today?*

Overall, remember that your clincher should feel like the end of your essay and leave your reader feeling like they read something meaningful, either by bringing them back full circle to your introduction, showing them the larger ramifications of your topic, or inspiring them in some way. The next page contains a summary of these four types of clinchers.

Congratulations! You have all the basic knowledge for writing each paragraph of a standard essay. Keep in mind that there are many other skills that go into writing a strong essay, and we will get to these topics in the subsequent chapters of this book. Writing isn't just about knowing *what* to say, it's about knowing *how* to say it.

Type of Clincher	Questions to Consider	Example
Bookends	*What key words from my hook can I return to in my clincher?* *Did I start with a story I could finish or a question that needs answering?*	*Hook: What is the difference between a job and a career?* *Clincher: Being a doctor is more than a job to pay the bills, it is a career that inundates your whole life with meaning and purpose.*
So What?	*Why does your topic matter?* *Why is it an important issue?*	*These events led by King were instrumental in breaking down the barriers of segregation and injustice, and without them, the nation would not be what it is today.*
Broader Implications	*How does this topic affect the larger world around us?*	*King's powerful campaign transcends time and place, spurring change not only the United States, but around the world.*
Call to Action	*What should we do with this information?*	*Every choice matters. By choosing to act with virtue, honesty, and integrity in all situations everyone can help their community flourish.*

Reading Comprehension Questions

1. Why should you avoid "this is" at the start of the conclusion paragraph?

2. What is the clincher, and what is its purpose?

ACTIVITY

Crafting Strong Clinchers / Practice

Each thesis below shows you generally what the essay was about. Using that information, try to craft a strong clincher sentence. After you have written it, identify the type you think it most closely resembles. If the thesis contains first or second person, you may use first or second person in your clincher, but otherwise try to write in third person.

1. Schools should not assign homework because it does not significantly increase test scores, it causes unneeded stress, and it inhibits beneficial extracurricular activities.

Clincher: ______________________________

____

____

2. Students should have homework because it provides extra practice, prepares them for adulthood, and encourages self-reliance.

Clincher: ______________________________

____

____

3. I admire my father because he is kind to everyone and supportive of all my endeavors.

Clincher: ______________________________

____

____

4. Piano serves as the best first instrument because of its versatility and availability.

Clincher: ______________________________

____

____

ACTIVITY

Crafting Strong Clinchers / Practice

Each thesis below shows you generally what the essay was about. Using that information, try to craft a strong clincher sentence. After you have written it, identify the type you think it most closely resembles. If the thesis contains first or second person, you may use first or second person in your clincher, but otherwise try to write in third person.

5. Reading fiction books not only entertains us but also helps improve our imagination, vocabulary, and understanding of people different from us.

Clincher: ______________________________

____

____

6. The ancient Egyptian civilization made significant contributions to architecture, writing, and mathematics.

Clincher: ______________________________

____

____

7. Participating in team sports teaches valuable life skills such as cooperation, discipline, and perseverance that can benefit students both on and off the field.

Clincher: ______________________________

____

____

8. All children should have a pet because it brings companionship, love, and health benefits to the whole family.

Clincher: ______________________________

____

____

Essay Writing / Putting it all together

Now that we have gone over all the main elements of the essay, let's write one! Using one of the essay maps you created in Chapter 3, write a five-paragraph essay. Below you will see a summary of what sentences should be written for each paragraph. Use this to help you and reference the earlier chapters as needed. Use the following pages to begin writing your essay.

Paragraph 1: The Introduction (from Chapter 4)	
Sentence:	***Explanation:***
1	**Hook:** A sentence that catches your reader's attention. Questions, interesting facts, anecdotes, quotations, and metaphors can all make good hooks.
2	**Connecting Sentence:** A sentence to lead from your hook to your thesis
3	**Thesis Statement:** 1-2 sentences that presents your claim about the topic and your three main points. You should have already created this, so now you just have to type it down again.

Paragraph 2: Body Paragraph 1 (from Chapter 5)	
Sentence	***Explanation:***
1	**Claim:** A sentence which states your topic and your first main point (i.e. "I want to be a teacher because I want to inspire my students.")
Varies	**Evidence:** A sentence to prove your claim. There can be multiple evidence sentences.
Varies	**Analysis:** A sentence to explain your evidence.
Last sentence	**Wrap-up:** A sentence to restate or summarize the main point of this paragraph and may also provide a transition to the next point.

Paragraph 3: Body Paragraph 2
Repeat above steps for 2nd main point

Paragraph 4: Body Paragraph 3
Repeat above steps for 3rd main point

Paragraph 5: The Conclusion (from Chapter 6)	
Sentence:	***Explanation:***
1-2	**Summary:** Two sentences that summarize the main points of your essay. It should be slightly more detailed than your thesis.
3	**Clincher:** The final sentence of your essay that gives a meaningful send-off to your reader. Some types of clinchers include creating bookends by complementing your hook, answering the question "So what?" about your argument, considering the broader implications of your argument, or giving your reader a "Call to Action."

ESSAY

5-Paragraph Essay / Rough Draft

Use the space below and on the next two pages to write your rough draft based on the essay map you chose from Chapter 3. Reference the chart on the previous page as needed. Indent the beginning of each pagraph. When you finish a paragraph and are ready to start a new one, go to the next line and indent before you begin writing. Focus on writing in complete sentences and getting your ideas down on paper.

ESSAY

ESSAY

ESSAY

Self-Evaluation / 5-paragraph Essay

Use this evaluation rubric to score your essay in each of the categories we have discussed. In each blank, give yourself a score out of three points. Put a zero if you forgot to do that part at all. In the reflection column, explain why you gave yourself that score. Be thoughtful and honest in your reflection — that is how you are going to improve.

Essay Component	*Criteria*		*Reflection*
Introduction 3 points each _____ / 9 points	_____ Hook _____ Connecting hook to thesis _____ Thesis statement		
1st Body Paragraph 3 points each _____ / 12 points	____ Claim ____ Evidence	____ Analysis ____ Wrap-up	
2nd Body Paragraph 3 points each _____ / 12 points	____ Claim ____ Evidence	____ Analysis ____ Wrap-up	
3rd Body Paragraph 3 points each _____ / 12 points	____ Claim ____ Evidence	____ Analysis ____ Wrap-up	
Conclusion 3 points each _____ / 6 points	_____ Summary _____ Clincher		

TOTAL: ______/51

ESSAY

Essay Writing / Putting it all together

Let's write on a new prompt from start to finish. Use the following prompt to brainstorm, form a thesis, create an essay map, and write your essay. All the worksheets have been provide for you. Begin below on your brainstorming.

Write a 5-paragraph essay on a dream you have for the future. It can be a specific goal you have, or a more general goal that would make the world a better place. Your body paragraphs can focus on why this is your dream or why the goal would make the world a better place.

Brainstorming Space:

ACTIVITY

Writing the Thesis Statement / Flowchart

Use the flowchart below to draft and revise your thesis statement.

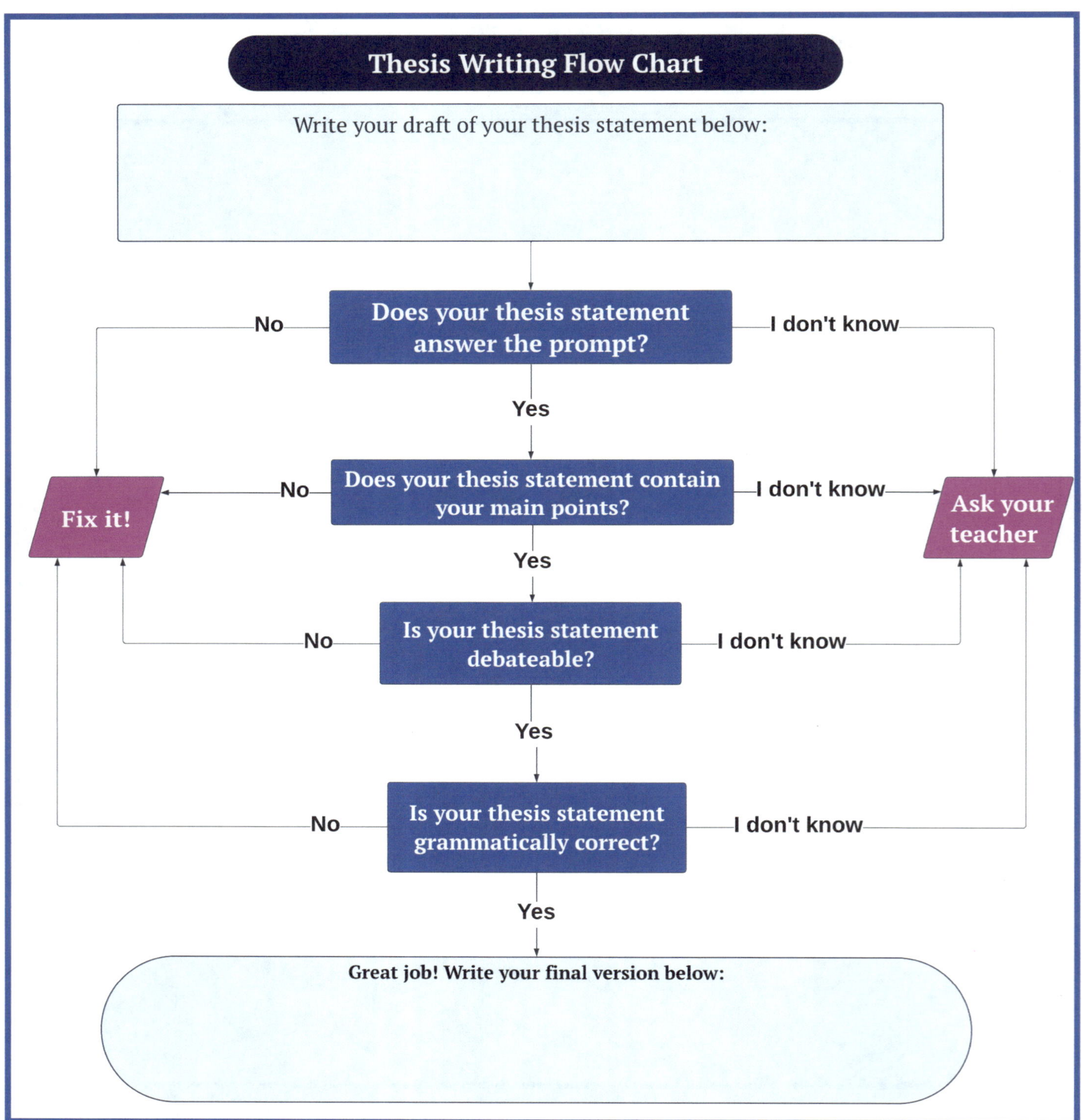

ACTIVITY

Essay Map

Use the following essay map to outline your essay based on the thesis you created on the previous page. Then, write your essay on the following pages.

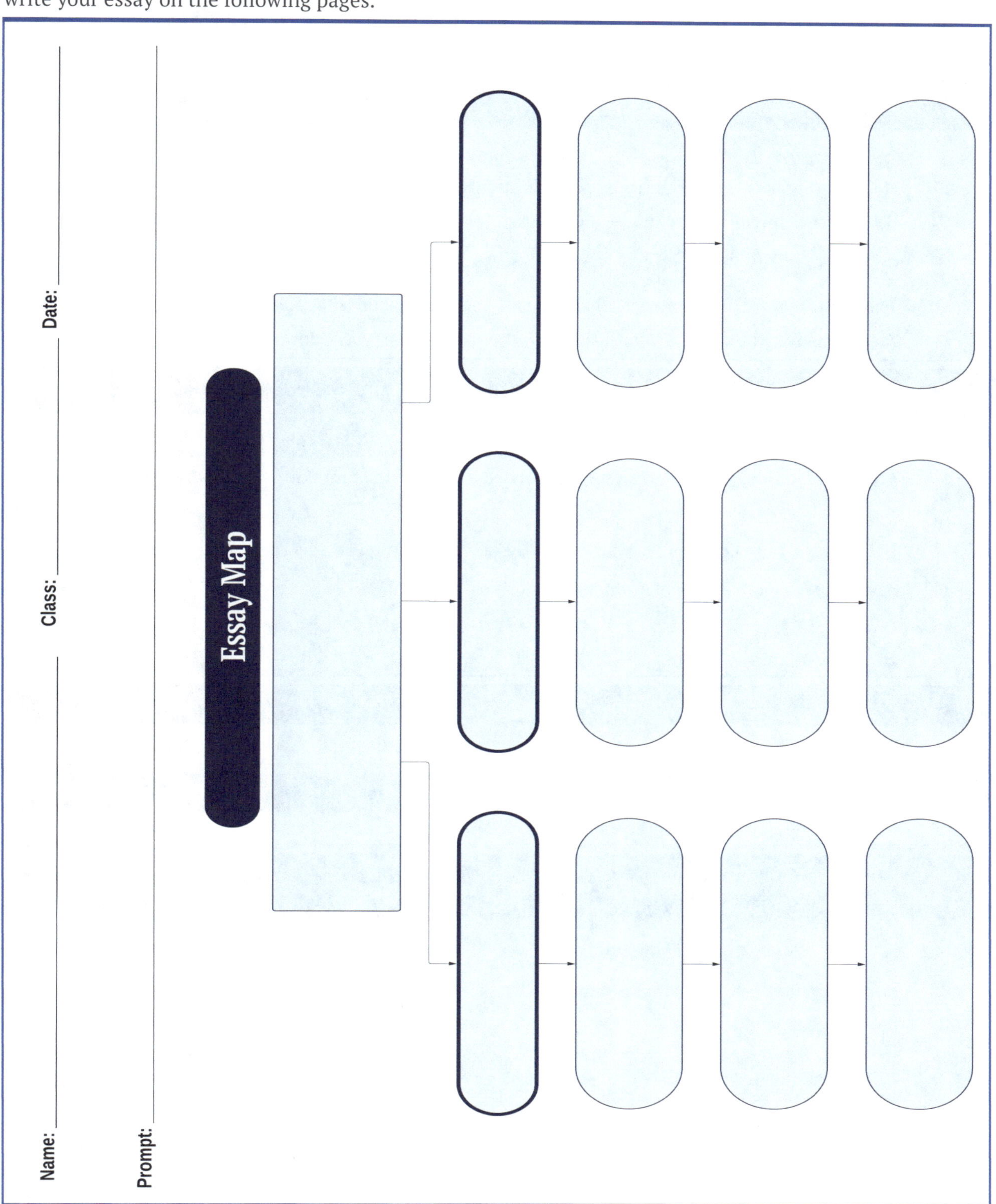

ESSAY

Essay Writing / Putting it all together

Now that we have gone over all the main elements of the essay, let's write one! Using one of the essay maps you created in Chapter 3, write a five-paragraph essay. Below you will see a summary of what sentences should be written for each paragraph. Use this to help you write your draft, and reference the earlier chapters as needed. Use the following pages to begin writing the draft of your essay.

Paragraph 1: The Introduction (from Chapter 4)	
Sentence:	***Explanation:***
1	**Hook:** A sentence that catches your reader's attention. Questions, interesting facts, anecdotes, quotations, and metaphors can all make good hooks.
2	**Connecting Sentence:** A sentence to lead from your hook to your thesis
3	**Thesis Statement:** 1-2 sentences that presents your claim about the topic and your three main points. You should have already created this, so now you just have to type it down again.

Paragraph 2: Body Paragraph 1 (from Chapter 5)	
Sentence	***Explanation:***
1	**Claim:** A sentence which states your topic and your first main point (i.e. "I want to be a teacher because I want to inspire my students.")
Varies	**Evidence:** A sentence to prove your claim. There can be multiple evidence sentences.
Varies	**Analysis:** A sentence to explain your evidence.
Last sentence	**Wrap-up:** A sentence to restate or summarize the main point of this paragraph and may also provide a transition to the next point.

Paragraph 3: Body Paragraph 2
REPEAT ABOVE STEPS FOR 2ND MAIN POINT

Paragraph 4: Body Paragraph 3
REPEAT ABOVE STEPS FOR 3RD MAIN POINT

Paragraph 5: The Conclusion (from Chapter 6)	
Sentence:	***Explanation:***
1-2	**Summary:** Two sentences that summarize the main points of your essay. It should be slightly more detailed than your thesis.
3	**Clincher:** The final sentence of your essay that gives a meaningful send-off to your reader. Some types of clinchers include creating bookends by complementing your hook, answering the question "So what?" about your argument, considering the broader implications of your argument, or giving your reader a "Call to Action."

5-Paragraph Essay / Rough Draft

Use the space below and on the next two pages to write your rough draft based on the essay map you chose from Chapter 3. Reference the chart on the previous page as needed. Indent the beginning of each pagraph. When you finish a paragraph and are ready to start a new one, go to the next line and indent before you begin writing. Focus on writing in complete sentences and getting your ideas down on paper.

ESSAY

ESSAY

Self-Evaluation / 5-paragraph Essay

Use this evaluation rubric to score your essay in each of the categories we have discussed. In each blank, give yourself a score out of three points. Put a zero if you forgot to do that part at all. In the reflection column, explain why you gave yourself that score. Be thoughtful and honest in your reflection - that is how you are going to improve.

Essay Component	*Criteria*	*Reflection*
Introduction 3 points each _____ / 9 points	_____ Hook _____ Connecting hook to thesis _____ Thesis statement	
1st Body Paragraph 3 points each _____ / 12 points	____ Claim ____ Analysis ____ Evidence ____ Wrap-up	
2nd Body Paragraph 3 points each _____ / 12 points	____ Claim ____ Analysis ____ Evidence ____ Wrap-up	
3rd Body Paragraph 3 points each _____ / 12 points	____ Claim ____ Analysis ____ Evidence ____ Wrap-up	
Conclusion 3 points each _____ / 6 points	_____ Summary _____ Clincher	

TOTAL: ______/51

ESSAY

Peer Evaluation / 5-paragraph Essay

Use this evaluation rubric to score the content of your partner's draft in each of the categories. In each blank, give them a score out of three points. Put a zero if they forgot to do that part at all Be thoughtful and honest in your reflection - that is how you are going to help them improve. In the explanation column, explain why you gave them that score

Essay Component	*Criteria*	*Explanation*
Introduction 3 points each _____ / 9 points	_____ Hook _____ Connecting hook to thesis _____ Thesis statement	
1st Body Paragraph 3 points each _____ / 12 points	____ Claim ____ Analysis ____ Evidence ____ Wrap-up	
2nd Body Paragraph 3 points each _____ / 12 points	____ Claim ____ Analysis ____ Evidence ____ Wrap-up	
3rd Body Paragraph 3 points each _____ / 12 points	____ Claim ____ Analysis ____ Evidence ____ Wrap-up	
Conclusion 3 points each _____ / 6 points	_____ Summary _____ Clincher	

TOTAL: ______/51

Artwork

Section III Enhancing Your Writing

CHAPTERS

TRINITY COLLEGE

Libraries provide a prime example of the importance of organization. Not only do their systems allow you to easily find the particular book you need, but they are also organized in a logical way that allows you to browse for similar books. After the earth science & geology section, you will find fossils & prehistoric life, followed by life sciences & biology. In the same way that the topics on the library's shelf lead from one to the next, so too your paragraphs should lead naturally from one idea to the next.

By Sylvain Tanguy

CHAPTER 7

Improving Organization

ROADMAP

- Identify irrelevant sentences in a paragraph.
- Learn how to restructure your paragraphs to flow more logically.
- Explore the various ways to logically order your paragraphs.
- Practice rearranging sentences and adding transitions.

THALES OUTCOME
Nº 13

Having **Well-developed People & Communication Skills** *allows for more effective sharing with a clear message.*

Improving your essay's organization is essential to crafting a strong essay. Without a clear, organized message, your audience will not be able to follow your ideas, and the whole argument will fall apart.

Organizing Your Essay

NOW THAT YOU KNOW the basics of writing each paragraph in an essay, it is time to improve them. Getting all your sentences and paragraphs on paper is a great first step, but you are far from finished. Essays require extensive editing before they are complete. In the following chapters, we will discuss how to revise three main elements of your essay: the organization, the word choice, and the sentence structure.

Organization within your essay is more difficult than it may sound. When you are first writing, you may write in "**stream of consciousness**," which is when people write or speak the thoughts as they think them — and not necessarily in a logical or organized manner. By beginning with a brainstorming web and essay map, you have taken the first step to organizing your writing because you have already grouped your ideas into key points. When you wrote the sentences of your rough draft, though, you may have added additional sentences as new ideas came to you or changed your direction slightly as you thought more deeply about your topic.

A well-organized essay meets three primary requirements: each paragraph only discusses one idea, each sentence follows logically from the one before, and transition words and phrases help sentences and paragraphs flow smoothly from one to the next.

Simply dividing your essay into paragraphs is the first step in having an organized essay. Remember that a paragraph is a group of sentences with one main idea that supports the thesis. Always go down to the next line and **indent** the start of a paragraph to show the reader a new paragraph has begun. Indenting is when you move the beginning of a line to the right about half an inch. When typing, this is done by pressing the tab key once or the space bar 7-10 times.

When revising, begin by finding the claim sentence of your first body paragraph. Remember, the very first paragraph should be your introduction, so your first body paragraph will actually be the second paragraph of your essay. Read through your claim and make sure it gives one clear reason that supports your thesis statement. If it does, the next step is to read through the rest of the paragraph sentence-by-sentence, checking that each one supports that claim and does not veer off-topic.

Irrelevant Sentences

Let's examine a paragraph that needs to be revised. While you are reading, see if you can spot the irrelevant sentences that need to be removed (the sentences in the paragraph have been numbered to more easily identify each one).

To improve the organization of your essay, make sure that each paragraph only focuses on one claim and that each sentence flows smoothly from one to the next by using logical reasoning and transition words and phrases.

Vocabulary

Indent
Moving the beginning of a line to the right about half an inch. When typing this is done by pressing the tab key once or the space bar 7-10 times.

Stream of Consciousness
Writing or speaking as the thoughts come to you with no particular order or organization.

Transitions
Words or phrases such as "next" or "on the other hand" that help the reader move from one sentence or idea to the next.

1. Students should establish their study space away from the main living area where they may be distracted by siblings, pets, and screens. 2. Too much screen time is detrimental to students' learning. 3. Students should sit in a supportive chair at a desk or table. 4. A comfortable but firm chair encourages a good posture and is more conducive to studying. 5. Finding an effective study spot is key to a successful school year. 6. Making effective use of study hall time will help students avoid being overwhelmed by homework. 7. A calendar is a useful way to keep track of assignments. 8. Quality study spots should be free of distractions. 9. The study space should be comfortable, but not too comfortable. 10. They should leave any phones or other devices in a separate room.

Now, there are multiple issues in the organization of this paragraph, but we will begin with the idea of relevance. After analyzing the above paragraph, we can see that the general argument of the paragraph is that an effective study space leads to a successful student. The sentence that most exemplifies this idea is the fifth sentence: ***Finding an effective study spot is key to a successful school year.*** Now, re-read the paragraph. Do you see any sentences that do not explain or support this idea?

The second, sixth, and seventh sentences are all irrelevant to finding an effective study spot. The second focuses on the harms of screen time, the sixth discusses using study hall time, and the seventh mentions using calendars to track assignments. None of these sentences explain or analyze what makes an effective study space. When revising your own paragraphs, if you come across a sentence that is not relevant but you still believe contains important information, that may mean that you should develop that idea in a different paragraph. For example, the sentence above about the usefulness of a planner could be the start of a separate paragraph in a larger essay about how to be a successful student. Let us re-number the sentences of our paragraph now that we have eliminated the irrelevant sentences:

1. Students should establish their study space away from the main living area where they may be distracted by siblings, pets, and screens. 2. Students should sit in a supportive chair at a desk or table. 3. A comfortable but firm chair encourages a good posture and is more conducive to studying. 4. Finding an effective study spot is key to a successful school year. 5. Quality study spots should be free of distractions. 6. The study space should be comfortable, but not too comfortable. 7. They should leave any phones or other devices in a separate room.

Sentence Order

After removing any irrelevant sentences, we want to put the sentences in a better order. Make sure the claim sentence is first, then group the remaining sentences into related ideas and make sure the sentences flow logically from one sentence to the next.

In our example, the author lists two main characteristics of effective study spaces — distraction-free and comfortable — as seen in sentences 5 and 6 on the previous page. Sentences 1 and 7 explain how to create a distraction-free study space while sentences 2 and 3 explain how to make the space comfortable. We should place the claim sentence (sentence 4) first, then group the remaining sentences into these two ideas, giving us a paragraph that looks like this:

Finding an effective study spot is key to a successful school year. Quality study spots should be free of distractions. Students should establish their study space away from the main living area where they may be distracted by siblings, pets, and screens. They should leave any phones or other devices in a separate room. The study space should be comfortable, but not too comfortable. Students should sit in a supportive chair at a desk or table. A comfortable but firm chair encourages a good posture and is more conducive to studying.

Transition Words

Another element for improving the organization of your paragraph (and your overall essay) is using transitions. Transitions are words and phrases like "in addition," "on the other hand," "therefore," and "secondly," which help guide the reader from point to point and improve your essay's overall flow. Transitions should be used both within and between paragraphs because they add clarity to your paper. The end of this chapter includes charts of various types of transition words and phrases to reference as you write. Let us demonstrate the addition of transitions with the same paragraph we've been using. Here is what our revised paragraph looks like:

Final body paragraph:

Finding an effective study spot is key to a successful school year. ***First****, quality study spots should be free of distractions. Students should establish their study space away from the main living area where they may be distracted by siblings, pets, and televisions. They should* ***also*** *leave any phones or other devices in a separate room.* ***Secondly****, the study space should be comfortable, but not too comfortable.* ***In particular****, students should sit in a supportive chair at a desk or table. This seating arrangement keeps them engaged and ultimately leads to more effective studying.*

We have bolded the transition words we added. These words help lead the reader from one point to the next. You will also usually start each paragraph with a transition word to lead from one main idea to the next. Very simple transition words could be "firstly" or "to begin with" for your first body paragraph. For the next paragraph, you may choose a transition like "secondly" or "in addition." You can also use an entire sentence to transition into the next paragraph by ending the first body paragraph with a transition sentence as we discussed in Chapter 5. Again, this technique is more advanced, and we will not go into more detail at this time.

Paragraph Order

The final element we will discuss regarding the organization of your essay is the way you choose to order your paragraphs. You could actually determine the order of your body paragraphs while working on your essay map; you do not need to wait for the revision stage to consciously choose what order to arrange your paragraphs.

There are three different ways to order your body paragraphs: in chronological order, in order of importance, or in logical order. If you are writing a report on John Adams, for instance, and your paragraphs discuss his early life, his education, and his achievements, a chronological order works well since his early life happened before he went to university and his most notable achievements happened after. This choice allows your ideas to naturally flow from one to the next. If you end up talking about his marriage in the paragraph on his "early life" and his childhood education in the second paragraph on "education," the arrangement of ideas is no longer chronological and will not flow as well. Instead, leave his marriage out of your essay and focus on his time at Harvard when discussing his education. *(Note: If these other areas are important to your overall thesis, such as if you want to discuss his many letters to his wife, a different organizational method might work better for your essay.)*

On the other hand, if each of your paragraphs is focused on a different one of John Adams's achievements, you might choose to order them by their importance. When ordering by importance, you should usually save the best for last — putting the one that you consider most important final — since that will be what people remember most clearly at the end of your essay. What you find most important may even be a part of your argument. Which is more important to you, John Adams' work on the Treaty of Paris to end the American Revolution or his time as second president of the United States?

The final way to order your paragraphs would be logically, meaning that one paragraph seems to flow naturally into the next. For instance, if you are writing your essay on the habits of a successful student, perhaps you end a paragraph about the study environment by talking about decorating the space with facts you need to memorize. This idea would logically lead into a paragraph about methods for studying for tests and quizzes. On the other hand, a paragraph on the importance of using a planner might lead into a paragraph about the study environment if you ended the paragraph by mentioning how you should always keep your planner on your desk.

Editing for organization is an important first step in revising your essay. You will want to edit for organization before revising for word choice and sentence structure because it often causes the biggest structural changes to your essay. After all, you may need to reorder entire paragraphs or remove sentences to improve the organization.

On the next page, you will find charts of transition words grouped by their purpose to help you organize your essays.

Transition Words/ Charts

To Show Addition		
Another	*Above all*	*Additionally*
Also	*To add to that*	*Once more*
Besides	*Equally important*	*Again*
Further	*In addition*	*Another*
Moreover	*Furthermore*	*Plus*

To Show Emphasis		
Above all	*More importantly*	*Certainly*
Primarily	*Significantly*	*Surely*
Chiefly	*Strikingly*	*Absolutely*
Notably	*Unequivocally*	*Finally*
Definitely	*First and foremost*	*Most of all*

To Indicate a Conclusion		
Thus	*In other words*	*Finally*
In short	*In summary*	*In closing*
All in all	*To summarize*	*Therefore*
Lastly	*In conclusion*	*As a result*

To Show Similarity		
Similarly	*In the same way*	*Likewise*

To Show Contrast		
But	*In contrast*	*Although*
Yet	*On the other hand*	*Conversely*
However	*Even though*	*Nevertheless*

To Show Time		
Next	*Suddenly*	*Frequently*
Then	*Occasionally*	*Repeatedly*
Before	*Temporarily*	*Often*
After	*Intermittently*	*Usually*
Meanwhile	*Periodically*	*Sporadically*
Earlier	*When*	*Momentarily*
First	*While*	*Later*
Second	*At the same time*	

There are many more words, phrases, and sentences that you can use to help with the organization and flow of your writing, but these will help get you started!

Reading Comprehension Questions

1. Why is editing for organization so important? Why should it be done first?

2. What do you need to check for in each paragraph to ensure it is well-organized?

3. Explain the different ways to order the paragraphs in your essay.

4. Where in your essay should you include transitions?

ACTIVITY

Revising Paragraphs / Practice

Instructions: The paragraphs below contain irrelevant sentences. Read through each paragraph carefully. Then, underline the claim sentence and cross out the irrelevant sentences.

1. One benefit of playing sports is that it teaches perseverance. When a player first tries a new sport, they will often struggle. They may not be strong enough to serve the ball over the net or agile enough to swerve around another player. One of the most challenging sports is ice hockey. However, when players persevere, they work through these struggles, becoming stronger and more agile each day. Even more experienced players will always have new skills to acquire or improve. By sprinting often, players can improve their speed, and by lifting weights, they can improve their strength. By participating in athletics, players can recognize their improvements and see the value of perseverance.

2. One way to succeed in school is to use a planner or agenda. A planner helps students keep track of due dates and stay organized with their time. Most students' favorite time of day is when they have finished their homework. By using a planner, students visualize each activity in their day and can plan accordingly. Having an extracurricular activity helps students learn to work together. If they notice that they have a test on Thursday and Friday, they know that they need to plan ahead to begin studying. An organized student is a successful student.

3. Being a clear communicator is essential in every occupation. Without strong communication skills, nothing can get done. Nurses need to communicate with their patients, and their patients need to communicate with them. Then, the nurses pass those messages on to the doctor to use in her diagnosis. Nurses and doctors work long hours. If there is a break in communication, those jobs cannot get done.

ACTIVITY

Ordering Paragraphs / Practice

Instructions: Each question below lists a topic and a few main points. Imagine that those points each represent a body paragraph. Write out what order you would put those paragraphs in, which method you are using (in logical order, chronological order, or order of importance) and why. See the example for more details.

Example: Study Skills: Using a planner, studying for tests, staying organized

I would order these paragraphs logically in this order: staying organized, using a planner, and studying for tests. Staying organized is a broader topic and will lead into using a planner, and then ending with studying for tests because you will need your planner to keep track of those test.

1. Charles Dickens: his books, his childhood, his farewell readings

2. Ancient Rome: architecture, inventions, clothing

3. Einstein: theories, awards, early life

ESSAY

Journal Writing / Practice Makes Perfect

Let's practice writing with transitions and organization. Pick a fun day you've had recently and consider the things you did chronologically. Then, write a journal entry about what happened, making sure to use a variety of different transition words and phrases to lead your reader through your story. When you are done, go back and reread your work and revise for typos and grammar errors, and with your teacher's permission, share it with a classmate.

ESSAY

PLAGE À HEIST

Neo-impressionism is a form of art marked by many small dots of color that work together to form a detailed scene. Your word choice works in a similar way. Each word is very small but when they are put together they form the whole scene of the essay.

Painting by Georges Lemmen

CHAPTER

Improving Word Choice

ROADMAP

- Learn how to avoid vague words.
- Discover ways to add detail to your sentences.
- Explore the effect of word choice on your tone.
- Understand what words to avoid in formal writing.
- Practice revising sentence vocabulary.

THALES OUTCOME
Nº 6

A **Continuous Learner** *takes lessons from all aspects of life and work, learns from mistakes, and adapts to change.*

Improving the wording in your writing involves patience and dedication. You must first develop a more substantial vocabulary through extensive reading and practice. Then you must work painstakingly to choose every word in your writing with care and for a specific reason.

Improving Word Choice

NOW THAT YOU KNOW how to write and organize an essay's core paragraphs, it is time to work on making those paragraphs and sentences sound more precise and interesting. One way to make these improvements to your writing is through your vocabulary. The words you choose play a huge role in how effective, clear, and interesting your writing is. We talked about transition words last chapter, but now we will turn to all the other words in your essay as we learn how to revise your writing.

The first thing you want to do is get your ideas down on paper, as we practiced in previous chapters. Don't worry about your exact word choice while writing your initial draft. After you finish your first draft, then you revise. This process is slow and arduous but is essential for creating any quality piece of writing. You should read through your writing sentence-by-sentence and word-by-word, ensuring that you have chosen just the right word for each idea you want to convey. Every word in your essay should be chosen with care. However, your choice of words is not about proving that you know "big words." Each word you choose depends on the meaning, emotion, tone, and goal you want to accomplish with that word. Let's compare a few paragraphs that vary some of their words and discuss the effect that they have on the paragraph.

The man went down the road towards the town. It was nighttime. He saw someone across the street and went towards him.

This first example is very vague and leaves us with many questions. There is no emotion or feeling behind any of the words. The lack of feeling behind the language prevents us from becoming attached to this character or his story.

Here is a second example that keeps the same idea but changes the word choice:

The figure slithered out into the night, his motives shrouded in darkness. He slunk down the dimly lit alley, his eyes furtively scanning his surroundings. His gaze fell upon an unsuspecting soul. A chilling grin crept across his face as he crossed the street towards him.

This example evokes a sense of danger and fear. Words like "slithered," "shrouded," "slunk," and "chilling" all make the reader fear this man and the situation without anything harmful actually happening.

Every word in your essay should be chosen with a specific purpose in mind. Read through your writing one word at a time and choose every one of them with care.

Vocabulary

Thesaurus
A book that lists words with their synonyms grouped together.

Homonyms
Two words that are spelled and pronounced the same but have different meanings.

Connotation
The feeling associated with a word that goes beyond its literal dictionary definition.

Ambiguous
Something that is vague or unclear and therefore can have more than one meaning.

Imperative Sentence
A sentence that gives a command and uses the implied pronoun "you."

Interrogative Sentence
A sentence that asks a question.

Contraction
Two words reduced to one through use of an apostrophe, *i.e. can't, it's, we've, etc.*

Let's look at how different words create a less sinister example next:

> *The kind-faced man stepped out into the moonlit night. He strolled down the sidewalk, noticing the beauty of the stars dotting the sky. He smiled as he spotted his elderly neighbor, Mrs. Flamingo, out for her evening stroll with her Pomeranian, and he crossed the quiet street to say hello.*

This third example elicits more positive emotions. Instead of "slithering," this man simply "stepped." Instead of "slinking," he "strolled." These alternative words give a more calm, pleasant feeling to the paragraph.

Now, one final example:

> *The tall man rushed down the road, worry creasing his forehead. The moon rose higher in the sky as he dashed across the street waving frantically to his neighbor.*

In this final paragraph, we feel a stronger sense of urgency in the situation. Instead of "strolling," he's "rushing." Instead of calmly observing the twinkling stars, the movement of the moon emphasizes the quick passage of time.

As you can see from these examples, word choice makes quite a difference in the feelings that your paragraph evokes and how interesting it is to read. Just by choosing a few different words, our stories changed from boring to sinister and from peaceful to worrisome. Let's now look at some practical ways to improve the vocabulary in your writing.

Avoiding Vague Words

As a starting point for choosing your words with purpose, there are certain words that you should avoid whenever possible. These words are either vague or overused, and there is often a better, more precise word you can use in its place. One way to replace these words in your writing is by using a **thesaurus**. A thesaurus is like a dictionary, but instead of listing a definition for each word, it lists synonyms or similar words. Keep in mind that when using a thesaurus, you cannot just choose any word listed for the word you looked up. Consider the word "speak." When you look up synonyms for this word, you will probably find words like "chat," "shout," "tell," or "whisper." Although they are all forms of speaking, they all convey different meanings. You cannot simply replace one word with the other without considering the meaning of the word. ***The students whispered excitedly when they heard the news of the field trip*** conveys a very different meaning than ***The students shouted excitedly when they heard the news of the field trip.***

Now, choosing the correct replacement for the word "speak" may seem obvious because you know the meaning of all these words. However, imagine that you looked up a word and found a synonym that sounded interesting, but you didn't know its exact meaning. The sentence that you intended to write now means something different.

Consider some synonyms of "sad." Words you might come across in a thesaurus would be "depressed," "melancholy," and "pessimistic." Do you know the distinct meanings of each of these words? If you do, that's great! You have an excellent vocabulary. But if you do not, you may mistakenly believe that you could put any of these words in place of the word "sad", but it depends on the type of sadness. Pessimistic ("the tendency to expect only bad outcomes"), "melancholy" ("a gloomy state of mind, especially when habitual or prolonged"), and "depressed" ("sad and gloomy") all have slightly different meanings and therefore cannot be used interchangeably.

Another thing to be aware of when using a thesaurus is that many words have **homonyms**. Consider the word "trip." It can mean both "to go on an outing" and "to fall over something." A thesaurus will give a brief definition next to words that have homonyms so that you can be sure that you are looking at synonyms for the correct word. Otherwise, you might accidentally change a sentence from ***The boy tripped over his shoelaces*** to ***The boy voyaged over his shoelaces*** — not quite the same thing.

Beyond a word's dictionary definition, you must also consider a word's **connotation**. The connotation of a word is the undertone or general feeling of a word beyond its literal definition. One word may have a similar definition to another, but they are used in different circumstances and convey a very different emotion. Consider the words "childlike" and "childish." Both words are adjectives that mean characteristic of a child. In fact, Merriam-Webster defines them almost identically. It defines "childlike" as "resembling, suggesting, or appropriate to a child or childhood" and "childish" as "of, relating to, or befitting a child or childhood." However, their connotations differ dramatically.

The word "childlike" conveys a sense a playfulness and innocence while "childish" refers more to immaturity and foolishness. If someone says that an action "is very childlike," there is nothing negative associated with it. In fact, it may have been an action that was especially cute such as a toddler squealing with joy at their first experience of a playground slide.

On the other hand, an action deemed "childish" would be one that is considered immature based on the age of the child. An older child throwing a temper tantrum for not getting his way is childish. These are connotations that you need to be aware of. Dictionaries include many of their words in sample sentences to help convey these different connotations. Connotations can even vary by region and culture. Many of these connotations can be learned by reading these words in context, experiencing them in conversations, and asking questions. So, when you find a word in a thesaurus you want to use in place of a word in your essay, make sure you understand both its definition and its connotation before you add it.

The following pages present some words that you should avoid in your writing because they are often overused or **ambiguous**. An ambiguous word is one that is vague or unclear because it can have more than one meaning. To avoid these words, determine what additional information you want to convey and then try to find a new verb, adjective, or adverb that provides that additional meaning.

To begin with, here are some verbs to avoid:

Verbs to Avoid		
Like	*Go/Went*	*See/Look*
Get/Got	*Say/Said*	

Note: The verb "to be" is often overused and causes sentences to be in the passive voice. We will discuss passive voice in more detail in the future, but try to only use conjugations of this verb (is, are, etc) when it is absolutely necessary for a particular reason.

To avoid these verbs, think about what makes the thing that way. Try asking yourself "how" or "why" questions.

For example, in the sentence, "The man went to the store" ask yourself "How did the man go?" Did he "dash," "wander," or "saunter"? "Dash" implies that he was hurrying quickly, "wander" implies slow movement with a lack of purpose, and "saunter" implies that he walked with pride and high self-esteem. The end of this chapter provides a chart of various alternatives to get you started finding replacements for these words in your writing.

There are also many adjectives that you should try to steer clear of:

Adjectives to Avoid		
Nice	*Awful*	*Big*
Wonderful	*Bad*	*Small*
Super	*Terrible*	

Again, these adjectives are very vague. All of them either refer to something's general size, or that it was good or bad, but it does not convey why. "Terrible" may sound like a better word than "bad," but ultimately it just means "very bad." Instead, try to find words that imply its quality while also providing additional information. Instead of ***The movie was terrible***, think about why it was terrible. Did the special effects appear fake, did the acting feel artificial, or was the plot boring? All of these ideas avoid merely declaring that the movie was "bad," "terrible," or "awful." Improve a sentence like ***The soccer game was great*** by asking yourself why it was great. Perhaps it was ***exciting*** or ***nerve-wracking***, so you can replace ***great*** with one of these more specific choices. By avoiding the words in the previous list, your writing becomes more detailed and interesting.

There are a few adverbs to try to avoid in your writing as well because they are overused. When you have so many words to choose from in the English language, there is often a more precise word for what you are trying to say.

Adverbs to Avoid		
Really	*Very*	*Not*

Instead of using words like "very" and "really," try to find a word that provides emphasis on its own, without the need of these words. For instance, rather than writing ***The soccer game was really exciting***, say ***The soccer game was thrilling***. The adjective "thrilling" means "really exciting" thereby cutting out an unnecessary word.

Also avoid "not" when possible. Only use it when you specifically need to indicate the absence of something. Instead, use the negative version of whichever word follows the word "not." Instead of ***The soccer game was*** *not exciting* say *The soccer game was boring* or *The soccer game was uneventful.*

Finally, there are a few other miscellaneous words that you must avoid in your writing at all costs:

Other Words to Avoid		
Stuff	*Thing(s)*	*Etc.*

These words provide no meaning. "Stuff" and "thing" can refer to almost any object in the world. You cannot simply look these words up in the thesaurus and find an alternative either. It is up to you to determine what the "stuff" or "things" are and to write about that instead. In the sentence *There are many things that students have to keep track of in middle school* you can replace "things" with "supplies," or even better, list some of those supplies by writing *Middle school students have to keep track of books, notebooks, pens, pencils, and an agenda, in addition to their actual homework.*

The abbreviation "etc." stands for et cetera and provides a way to abbreviate a list. However, there is no need for this abbreviation in formal writing. Use words to explain the information rather than taking a shortcut by just ending your list with "etc." Instead of *Students need pens, pencils, paper, notebooks, etc.*, you could say *Students need many supplies including pens, pencils, paper, notebooks, binders, and looseleaf paper.* You could also revise the sentence by saying, *Students need supplies such as pens, pencils, and notebooks.* By using the phrase "such as," the author implies that this list is incomplete and can include other items without the use of "etc."

Avoiding "To Be" Verbs

In your writing, try to avoid unnecessary "to be" verbs. These include *am*, *is*, *are*, *was*, *were*, *be*, *being*, *and been*. Your writing will generally be more effective by avoiding these words and using strong, active verbs instead.

Let's look at some examples of weak and strong sentences:

Weak	Strong
Thomas Edison was known for the light bulb. *This sentences contains the "to be" verb "was" and is more wordy than necessary.*	*Thomas Edison invented the light bulb.* *This sentence uses the action verb "invented" and is stronger and more direct.*
Cardiovascular health is improved by exercise. *This sentence contains the "to be" verb "is" and is more wordy than necessary.*	*Exercise improves cardiovascular health.* *This sentence uses the action verb "improves" which strengthens the sentence.*

Avoiding forms of the verb "to be" strengthens your sentence by making it less wordy and allowing for more effective, precise verbs. We will discuss this concept further in Chapter 10 on descriptive writing.

Don't Write About Your Writing

One common area where students tend to struggle is a tendency to "write about their writing." This refers to including phrases such as *I will tell you*, *The first reason is*, or *This essay is about*. We discussed this wording briefly in Chapter 2 and Chapter 5 when we discussed thesis statements and claims. You may have been encouraged to write this way in the past as you first learned how to compose essays, but now that you have had at least a few years of practice, it is time to avoid these kinds of phrases. We know you are writing an essay. Instead of telling us that you will be telling us about something, simply provide the information. Instead of telling us *The first reason is*, simply give your first claim. (Remember how we talked about referring to the first sentence of a paragraph as a claim instead of a topic sentence? Using the term "claim" will remind you to avoid these phrases.)

Overall, you should avoid these words in your writing:

Writing Words to Avoid		
Point	*Reason*	*Essay*

There is no need to say *One reason students should study abroad is to gain first-hand knowledge of other cultures.* You should just state the claim: *Students should study abroad to gain first-hand knowledge of other cultures.* (Notice how this revision also avoids the dreaded "to be" verb, "is.") Again, do not say *My first point is about teamwork*, simply provide the claim: *Students should play sports because it teaches teamwork.*

Now, these words are okay when used in the argument of the essay itself. For example, there is nothing wrong with *The point of the Eiffel Tower reaches a staggering 1,083 feet.* This refers to a point on the tower, not to a point you will make in your essay. It would also be fine to say *Aristotle believed man's ability to reason set him apart from animals* since this sentence uses "reason" as part of its main information, not one of the "reasons" in support of your thesis.

Adding Details

The other way to improve the vocabulary in your writing is by adding descriptive words such as adjectives and adverbs. These words help your sentences come alive by painting a picture in the reader's mind. A sentence like *The lady walked through the woods* tells us what's happening but not much more. Instead, by adding more descriptive details, we can really set the scene: *The elegant young lady drifted through the woods, her lithe body gliding nearly silently across the forest floor.* This sentence is more interesting and gives us a much clearer picture of what is happening.

Take a look at this short paragraph:

> *Cheetahs are large felines. They live in the Africa. They are known for being very fast.*

Notice how vague these words are. We can't really picture what cheetahs are like from this. How large are they? How fast? Where in Africa? We can improve these simple, choppy sentences by using more precise vocabulary and adding more detailed information. Words like "large" and "fast" are ambiguous; they are vague words, often open to interpretation. In comparison to a sparrow, an eagle is large; in comparison to a tortoise, a hare is quite fast. If we were not already familiar with cheetahs, being told that they are "large" and "fast" does not paint a very clear picture for us. Instead of ambiguous words like these, we can describe their size and speed. Let's take a look at a revised paragraph:

> *Cheetahs, members of the feline family, can weigh between 77 and 143 pounds. They primarily live in the open grasslands of Africa. Famous for their speed, they can reach 60 miles per hour in three seconds flat!*

Notice how, instead of simply saying that they are "large," we have given their weight, and instead of saying "fast," we have given their potential speed.

Another way you can improve these sorts of words would be through a comparison. Perhaps you can say *Cheetahs can reach 60 miles per hour, that's as fast as most cars on the highway!*

The use of active verbs also changed in our revisions between our first example and our second. In our first example, the first and last sentence both use the linking verb "are." When we revised the paragraph, instead of saying they *are large felines*, we used a modifying phrase *members of the feline family* and used the active verb phrase *can weigh*. As we discussed, avoiding the "to be" verb makes your sentences more powerful. As you become a more proficient writer, you will want to avoid this verb unless you need it for a specific reason.

Formal Writing

There are a couple more elements to pay attention to regarding formal essay writing: writing in third person and avoiding contractions. In our chapter on thesis statements, we discussed both of these elements, but it is important that you continue to follow these requirements in all your sentences, not just your thesis statement. First, let's review first, second, and third person.

As we discussed earlier, all pronouns are either first, second, or third-person pronouns. First-person refers to pronouns that include the speaker, like *I*, *me*, or *us*. Second-person pronouns are ones that refer to the audience you are speaking to, like *you* and *yours*. Third-person pronouns are the ones that refer to other people or things like *they*, *he*, or *it*. Generally, in formal essays, you should only use third-person point of view, meaning that it should not contain any *you* or *I* words. Writing in the first or second person is seen as more informal and should not be used in formal essays. (For a chart of the different pronouns, see chapter 2.)

Recall also that **imperative sentences** are second person sentences because they have the implied pronoun *you*. These sentences make a command like *Pay close attention to your word choice*.

If you find yourself accidentally including first or second person pronouns in your writing, keep in mind that this issue involves the structure of your sentence. Usually, you cannot simply replace one word with another to fix these kinds of sentences — you need to re-write the sentence altogether. Let's look at some examples.

The sentence *I will tell you about the effects of greed* is written in first person. This could be fixed by making a claim instead of telling the audience that you will be telling them something. Instead say, *Greed harms the world in many ways* or *Many harmful consequences result from greed.*

Imperative sentences often need to be entirely replaced to avoid second person in your essay. For instance, the imperative sentence *Imagine a world without music* cannot be changed to third person by just substituting or taking out a word. Instead of this sentence, state a fact such as *A world without music would be incredibly dreary.*

Interrogative sentences are sentences that ask a question. When they are written in second person, they also cannot simply be fixed with a substitution. Instead of an interrogative sentence like *What do you do for fun?* figure out why you are wanting to ask this question and give direct information instead. Are you about to write a personal essay on your favorite activity? Instead, give a fact about it — *Water skiing is a thrilling sport that is both challenging and invigorating.* Are you asking the question in order to discuss various popular activities? Instead, give a statistic like *The most popular hobby in the U.S. in 2024 was cooking or baking (Bashir).* Really, you should avoid questions in formal writing altogether unless absolutely necessary even if they do not contain second person because they are already considered informal.

Other sentences in the second person can be fixed by using a general third-person noun. For example, the sentence *Playing a team sport will help you learn cooperation* could instead read *Playing a team sport helps people learn cooperation* or *Playing a team sport teaches children cooperation.*

The other element that you must avoid in formal writing is **contractions**. Contractions are two words reduced to one through use of the apostrophe. Words like *can't*, *don't*, *we're*, *she'll* and *it's* are just a few of the many contractions in English. Luckily, contractions are incredible easy to fix! All you have to do is write out the contraction as two words. Instead of *she'll*, write *she will*; instead of *don't*, write *do not*; instead of *it's*, write *it is* and so forth.

Overall, when it comes to improving the vocabulary in your writing, remember that every word in your sentence matters. It won't be easy, but you must try to choose the most precise and interesting word you can in every sentence in order to have the strongest writing possible. Use a thesaurus to help you, but do so with caution and care; make your claims with confidence rather than writing about your writing; and make sure to use formal language when needed.

Now that you have some strategies for improving your vocabulary, let's practice applying them. Below is a chart to help you avoid the vague verbs we discussed earlier.

Like/Love	*Go/Went*	*See/Look*	*Get/Got*	*Say/Said*
Enjoy	Proceed	Detect	Grab	Announce
Adore	Travel	Examine	Obtain	Answer
Cherish	Journey	Identify	Receive	Assert
Fancy	Adventure	Notice	Secure	Claim
Appreciate	Progress	Observe	Snag	Respond
Admire	Retire	Recognize	Capture	Suggest
Prefer	Flee	Regard	Apprehend	Reveal
Desire	Saunter	Peer	Seize	Mention
Elect	Stroll	Scan	Collect	Declare
Wish	Dash	Scrutinize	Earn	Estimate
Savor	Slitter	Gawk	Pocket	Voice
Treasure	Crawl	Glare	Accept	Allege
Relish	Hike	Inspect	Acquire	Divulge
Respect	Parade	Survey	Inherit	Relate
Prize	Traipse	Spy	Procure	Remark
Value	Roam	Note	Gain	Report
Honor	Trudge	Glimpse	Find	Reply
	Race	Study	Discover	
	Traverse	View	Locate	
	Rush		Unearth	
	Escape		Attain	
	Amble			
	Sprint			
	Depart			
	Hasten			

Reading Comprehension Questions

1. What do you have to be careful about when using a thesaurus?

2. Describe the different methods for improving your vocabulary in your writing.

3. What does "writing about writing" refer to? How can you avoid this tendency?

4. What additional words should you avoid in formal writing?

ACTIVITY

Improving Word Choice / Practice

Instructions: For each sentence below, re-write it with better vocabulary. Try to use action verbs, avoid vague language, and carefully use a thesaurus to improve the vocabulary in the sentence. You may add additional information to improve the sentence as long as it doesn't change the meaning. Make it the best sentence possible.

1. One reason to study a foreign language is to improve a student's understanding of grammar.

____

____

2. There are a lot of things that you have to remember to be a good student.

____

____

3. Fencing club is a great extracurricular activity because it is fun.

____

____

4. This essay is about being a good student.

____

____

5. The movie was terrible.

____

____

6. The food was great.

____

____

ACTIVITY

Improving Word Choice / Practice

Instructions: For each sentence below, re-write it with better vocabulary. Try to use action verbs, avoid vague language, and carefully use a thesaurus to improve the vocabulary in the sentence. You may add additional information to improve the sentence as long as it doesn't change the meaning. Make it the best sentence possible.

7. Being kind is something that everyone should do.

____

____

8. Dogs can be big or small.

____

____

9. I have told you about why we should have a four-day school week.

____

____

10. How to change a tire is an important thing to know.

____

____

11. *Charlotte's Web* is a book about many important lessons.

____

____

12. Rome had many different gods and goddesses.

____

____

ACTIVITY

Improving Word Choice / Practice

Instructions: For each sentence below, re-write it with better vocabulary. Try to use action verbs, avoid vague language, and carefully use a thesaurus to improve the vocabulary in the sentence. You may add additional information to improve the sentence as long as it doesn't change the meaning. Make it the best sentence possible.

13. Thomas Jefferson went to the College of William and Mary.

____

____

14. Persians had caravans to get supplies from one end of the plateau to the other.

____

____

15. The sunrise over the Blue Ridge Mountains is very pretty.

____

____

16. A tiger can move slowly to get his prey.

____

____

17. Tree frogs like warm and wet environments.

____

____

18. A hare is faster than a tortoise but in "The Tortoise and the Hare," the tortoise wins.

____

____

ACTIVITY

Writing in Formal Language / Practice

Instructions: Write out the following contractions in two words. For a couple of the questions, there may be more than one correct answer. Context is sometimes needed to determine the exact meaning of a contraction.

Contraction	*Written Out*	*Contraction*	*Written Out*	*Contraction*	*Written Out*
Example: Can't	*Cannot*				
1. Isn't		6. She's		11. I'm	
2. Don't		7. Won't		12. He'd	
3. We'll		8. They've		13. Shouldn't	
4. It's		9. Let's		14. Aren't	
5. They're		10. That's		15. Would've	

Instructions: Fill in the chart below for the first-person and second-person pronouns that you should avoid in formal writing. See Chapter 2 for reference.

First-person Pronouns	*Second-person Pronouns*

ACTIVITY

Writing in Formal Language / Practice

Instructions: For each sentence below, correct the sentence to be in third-person and free of contractions. You may add information as long as it does not contradict the information provided. Try to improve the general word choice when needed as well.

1. I think that everyone should learn to play an instrument because it teaches perseverance.

____

____

2. Think about how important study skills are.

____

____

3. Let's consider the reasons that sports are beneficial.

____

____

4. At the beginning of the play, Hamlet's convinced he sees his father's ghost.

____

____

5. When you learn a foreign language, you'll get better at English grammar, too.

____

____

6. If you want to succeed, it's important to put in good effort.

____

____

ACTIVITY

Writing in Formal Language / Practice

Instructions: Rewrite the paragraph below in formal language (third person, no contractions, minimal "to be" verbs, strong vocabulary, etc.).

What skill do you think is most important for school? I think the most important skill is organization. When you're organized, you can keep better track of your assignments and make sure you don't lose any. Being organized with your calendar will help you know when you have stuff coming up so you know what to study. Lastly, I think organization is important because you'll be able to plan your time better and have more time to relax.

ESSAY

Journal Writing / Practice Makes Perfect

Let's practice writing with a precise, detailed vocabulary. Pick something small that you can see, such as a book, a painting, a tree, or a car. Then, describe it in as much detail as you can. Don't worry about the structure of your sentences or writing a hook or a clincher, just focus on using the most precise, descriptive words you can. When you are done, go back and reread your work and revise for typos and grammar errors, and with your teacher's permission, share it with a classmate.

ESSAY

DOLOMITE ALPS

Like the mountains which rise and fall and vary so much in size and shape, so too should your sentences vary. Like these mountains, your sentences will vary in size and complexity, and they should rise and fall in rhythm like the peaks of a mountain.

Photo by jenyateua

CHAPTER

Improving Sentence Structure

ROADMAP

- Distinguish between the different sentence starters.
- Discover ways to vary the length of your sentences.
- Explore the effect of sentence length on your tone.
- Practice revising sentence structure.

THALES OUTCOME

Nº 10

A Strong Work Ethic *links perseverance, reliability, and honesty.*

Improving the structure of the sentences in your essay takes a lot of hard work and dedication. You cannot simply swap one word for another. Instead you must restructure the sentences entirely. By varying the structure of sentences throughout your essay, you improve the sound and rhythm of your essay, leading to a more enjoyable and memorable experience for your reader.

Improving Sentence Structure

SO FAR IN OUR CHAPTERS on revision, we have learned how to organize our writing and how to improve our writing with specific, strong words. Now we turn to improving the structure of our sentences. The structure of a sentence refers to the length, the complexity, and the order of the words within the sentence. There are two main reasons to edit the structure of your sentences:

1. To make your writing more eloquent, interesting, and beautiful.
2. To convey the tone and message of your writing more clearly.

First of all, an essay filled with sentences all written in the same structure is just boring. Imagine a row of houses each constructed in exactly the same way. Each house may be a different color, but an endless row of structurally identical houses is not as interesting or beautiful. Like the colors of the houses, the words of each sentence may change, but if the structure never varies, your reader will quickly tire of your essay and be less interested in your argument.

Now, keeping your reader interested has two benefits. One, they will want to keep reading to the end. If they get bored and stop halfway through, they never even read your whole argument. Two, what makes the writing interesting to the reader also makes it more memorable. Take a look at the short paragraph below:

87 years ago the nation was founded. It was founded on the idea of equality. We are engaged in civil war now. It will test whether the nation will endure.

Does this information sound familiar? It is a very simplified version of Abraham Lincoln's "Gettysburg Address." These sentences get the information across; they even have a few quality vocabulary words such as "founded," "engage," and "endure." However, they all have the same basic structure and come across very flat. Let us look at the actual first two sentences of the "Gettysburg Address":

Four score and seven years ago our fathers brought forth, upon this continent, a new nation, conceived in Liberty, and dedicated to the proposition that all men are created equal. Now we are engaged in a great civil war, testing whether that nation, or any nation so conceived, and so dedicated, can long endure.

The use of prepositional phrases, verbal phrases, adverbs, and conjunctions adds complexity to the

During revision, you should carefully analyze every sentence. By purposefully varying the structure of your sentences, you create a more beautiful piece of writing. When the sentences roll off the tongue more smoothly, your reader will become engrossed in your message and better remember your argument.

Vocabulary

Prepositions
Words that tell the relationship between a noun (the object of the preposition) and another word in the sentence.

Prepositional Phrase
A group of words beginning with a preposition and ending with the object of that preposition.

Adverb
Words that modify verbs, adjectives, or other adverbs.

Coordinating Conjunction
A word such as "and," "but," or "or," that connects words, phrases, or sentences of equal importance.

Subordinating Conjunction
A conjunction like "because" or "since" that begins a dependent clause.

Clause
A group of words with a subject and a verb.

Dependent Clause
Also known as a subordinating clause, this is a clause that begins with a subordinating conjunction and cannot stand by itself.

Independent Clause
A clause that makes sense by itself. Any simple sentence is an independent clause.

sentences. That complexity is part of what makes those sentences so memorable. Had Lincoln's speech been less eloquent, it would have merely presented the facts at hand, and it would not be the famous speech it is today.

Sentence Starters

One way to vary your sentence structure is by focusing on how you start your sentences. The simplest sentences are ones structured with the complete subject first, followed by the complete predicate. This structure is used in early reader books and is the way you are taught to construct sentences when you first learn to write. If you are writing a piece geared towards very young readers, you actually want to keep the sentences simple by starting each sentence with the subject. However, unless young children are your particular audience, using only subject starters is not the best way to write. Here is a paragraph written with all subject sentence starters:

> ***Albert Einstein*** *was born in Germany in 1879.* ***He*** *matriculated to the Swiss Federal Polytechnic School in Zurich in 1896 in order to become a physics and math teacher.* ***He*** *graduated in 1901, but he could not find a teaching job.* ***The patent office*** *hired him as technical assistant, and he used his free time to work on his theories.* ***He*** *was a distinguished professor throughout Switzerland and Germany.* ***He*** *moved to the United States in 1933.*

The complete subjects have been bolded for you. You can see that in this paragraph, each sentence begins with the complete subject; in fact, many begin with the exact same word. Notice that when we refer to the "subject" coming first, we are referring to the complete subject. In the fourth sentence, the sentence begins with the article "the" (an adjective); however, it is part of the complete subject.

Let's compare this paragraph to one that uses a variety of different sentence starters:

> ***Albert Einstein*** *was born in Germany in 1879.* ***In 1896,*** *he matriculated to the Swiss Federal Polytechnic School in Zurich in order to become a physics and math teacher.* ***Although he graduated in 1901,*** *he could not find a teaching job right away.* ***Instead,*** *he started a job at the patent office and used his free time to work on his most famous theories.* ***Soon,*** *universities recognized his groundbreaking work, and he became a distinguished professor throughout Switzerland and Germany.* ***In 1933,*** *he moved to the United States to be Professor of Theoretical Physics at Princeton, and the year of 1945 marked his official retirement.*

In the previous paragraph, you can see how the sentences are more eloquent, less choppy, and less simplistic. We have underlined the subjects (as you undoubtedly know, all sentences must have a subject) and bolded the sentence starters.

Here is a chart of each sentence of the paragraph and which kind of sentence starter it used:

Sentence Beginning	Opener type
Albert Einstein *was born in....*	*Subject*
In 1896, *he matriculated to the Swiss Federal Polytechnic School....*	*Prepositional phrase*
Although he graduated in 1901, *he could not find....*	*Subordinate clause*
Instead, *he started a job at....*	*Adverb*
Soon, *universities recognized his groundbreaking work...*	*Adverb*
In 1933, *he moved to the United States...*	*Prepositional Phrase*

As you can see, the sentences started with a variety of different structures including the subject, a prepositional phrase, a subordinating clause, and an adverb. Notice that sentences can still have subject starters, as shown above—you do not need to rid your essays of them entirely. Your job is to make sure to frequently vary which ones you use. An essay written entirely with prepositional phrase starters is scarcely better than one that uses all subject starters. A good rule is to have no more than two of the same sentence starter in a row and to have at least three or four different ones in each paragraph.

Now, you may not be familiar with some of these parts of speech we just mentioned, so we will review them before using these sentence starters in our writing.

Prepositional Phrases

You may already be familiar with **prepositions**. Prepositions are words that tell the relationship between a noun (the object of the preposition) and another

Vocabulary

Compound Sentence
Two independent clauses connected together with a comma and a coordinating conjunction to form one sentence.

Complex Sentence
A dependent clause connected to an independent clause using a subordinating conjunction.

Compound-Complex Sentence
A sentence containing three total clauses. Two of the clauses are joined by a coordinating conjunction, and two are joined by a subordinating conjunction.

Participle
A word that comes from a verb but is used as an adjective. It is also combined with helping verbs to form certain tenses.

Participial Phrase
A group of words that begins with either the past or present participle, followed by an object that goes with it. It always functions as an adjective.

Gerund
A word formed from a verb that acts at a noun in a sentence.

word in the sentence. Most prepositions, but not all, will fit into the sentence *The birds flew _______ the clouds.* For example, in the sentence *The birds flew around the clouds*, the word *around* is a preposition. To find the object of the preposition we ask, "Around what?" *Clouds* is the answer, making it the object of the preposition. A **prepositional phrase** begins at the preposition and ends at the object of the preposition; in the sentence above, the prepositional phrase is *around the clouds*. Here are some examples of sentences that use prepositional phrase starters:

Sentences with Preposition Starters	
***Throughout** the world, students study the works of William Shakespeare.*	*"Throughout the world" is a prepositional phrase. "Throughout" is a preposition and "world" is the object of the preposition.*
***On the other hand**, technology has infiltrated many aspects of our lives.*	*"On the other hand" is a prepositional phrase. "On" is a preposition and "hand" is the object of the preposition.*
***By the end** of his life, Charles Dickens had published 15 novels.*	*"By the end" is a prepositional phrase. "By" is a preposition and "end" is the object of the preposition.*

Now, if there is no object of the preposition, the word was never a preposition at all. For example, if the sentence said *The birds flew around* and we try to ask, "around what?" there is no answer. In this case, "around" is not a preposition; it is actually an adverb.

Adverbs

Adverbs modify verbs, adjectives, or other adverbs. They primarily answer questions beginning with "how," "when," "why," or "where." Many of the transition words we learned about in Chapter 7 were adverbs. Here are some sentences with adverb sentence starters:

Sentences with Adverb Starters	
***Meanwhile**, Albert Einstein continued work on his theories.*	*"Meanwhile" is an adverb that tells "when" about the verb "continued."*
***Each year**, millions of tourists visit Paris.*	*"Each year" tells "when" about the verb "visit."*
***Similarly**, Marie Curie faced hardships early in her career.*	*"Similarly" tells "how" about the verb "faced."*

Subordinating Conjunctions

You are probably already familiar with **coordinating conjunctions**. These are words like "and," "but," and "or." You may be less familiar with **subordinating conjunctions**. Here is a chart of the most common subordinating conjunctions:

Subordinating Conjunctions			
After	*Although*	*As*	*Because*
Before	*By the time*	*Even if*	*If*
Once	*Since*	*That*	*Though*
Unless	*Until*	*When*	*Whenever*
Where	*Whereas*	*Wherever*	*While*

You must be very careful when you use one of these words as a sentence starter. When you put a subordinating conjunction at the beginning of a sentence, you create a dependent clause. A **clause** is any group of words with a subject and a verb, but a **dependent clause** is one that does not make sense by itself. An **independent clause**, on the other hand, is one that makes sense by itself. Any simple sentence is an independent clause. To ensure that you have a complete sentence when you use a subordinating conjunction, you must have two clauses: a dependent clause and an independent clause. If you have a dependent clause by itself, it will be a fragment, not a complete sentence.

The chart below demonstrates the difference between an independent and dependent clause and a complete sentence versus a fragment:

Sentence	Explanation
It rarely rains in the Sahara. Plants must grow deep roots to find water.	*These are two complete sentences, or independent clauses. They can stand alone and make sense by themselves.*
***Since** it rarely rains in the Sahara.*	*This is a fragment. "Since" has turned the complete sentence into a dependent clause which cannot work by itself.*
Since *it rarely rains in the Sahara, plants must grow deep roots to find water.*	*This sentence is complete because the dependent clause is followed by an independent clause in the same sentence.*

From this chart you can see that just adding a subordinating conjunction to the beginning of a sentence turns a complete sentence into a sentence fragment. In your own writing, you cannot simply use a subordinating conjunction sentence starter by merely adding one of these words to the beginning of a sentence. You can correctly use them in one of two ways: you can take two of your sentences and combine them using a subordinating conjunction, or you can add an additional, new clause onto the sentence that started with the subordinating conjunction.

Here are some additional examples of sentences with subordinating conjunction sentence starters:

Sentences with Subordinating Conjunction Starters	
***Because the climate is so dry**, little vegetation can grow in the Sahara.*	*The first clause is a dependent clause because it has the subject and verb "climate is" but it begins with the subordinating conjunction "because." The second half of the sentence is an independent clause because it makes sense by itself and has the subject and verb "vegetation can grow."*
If students learn perseverance early, *they will struggle less in the future.*	*In this sentence, "if" is a subordinating conjunction, making the clause a dependent clause with the subject and verb "students learn." It is followed by an independent clause that would have made sense by itself with the subject and verb "they study."*

Confusing Words

Some words such as ***before***, ***after***, ***since***, ***around***, and many more can be adverbs, prepositions, or subordinating conjunctions. In order to determine how the word is being used in a particular sentence, you must always look at the context. Remember, a preposition will always have a noun that answers the question "what?" about it, a subordinating conjunction will start a clause that contains a subject and a verb, and an adverb will function by itself to describe a verb, adjective or other adverb.

Here is a chart demonstrating the same word used as different parts of speech depending on the sentence:

Sentence	Explanation
After grammar, students continue on to a study of logic.	*Here, "after" is being used as a preposition. We know this because it is followed by an object ("grammar"), not a subject and verb.*
After they study grammar, students will begin their study of logic.	*In this sentence, "after" is a subordinating conjunction. It is followed by a subject and verb "they study" which means it begins a clause.*
Outside, many people gathered to watch the eclipse.	*Here, "outside" is being used as an adverb. It does not have an object to go with it, and it answers the question "where" about the verb "gathered."*
Outside their homes, many people gathered to watch the eclipse.	*Here, "outside" is a preposition. We can ask "outside what?" to find the object of the preposition, in this case "homes."*

Varying Sentence Complexity

Besides using a variety of sentence starters, the other way to improve the structure of your sentences is by varying the sentence complexity. There are four main structures when it comes to the complexity of a sentence: simple, compound, complex, and compound-complex. A **simple sentence** is one with only one complete thought. Here are some examples:

Simple Sentences
Organization and time-management are essential skills.
Students and teachers alike must work hard and persevere through difficult situations.
After grammar, students begin their study of logic.

You will notice that there are some coordinating conjunctions in the sentences above, but there is only one complete thought in each. There is nowhere you could have divided either sentence into two ideas, so they are each just a simple sentence. The first sentence has a compound subject and the second has both a compound subject and compound predicate, but neither joins two complete sentences together.

A **compound sentence** is one that contains two independent clauses joined with a coordinating conjunction. They will have a complete thought before the conjunction and another complete thought after the conjunction. Let's take a look at some compound sentences:

Compound Sentences
In trivium, students study language, and they learn to write effectively.
Albert Einstein was born in 1879, and he died in 1955.
Albert Einstein received a Nobel Prize for his work in physics, but he is also known for his mathematical theories.

These are compound sentences because each contains two complete thoughts connected with a comma and coordinating conjunction between them. To check if you have a compound sentence, try imagining a period in place of a comma and conjunction. If you test that out with the above sentences, you will see that each could have been two short, simple sentences.

A **complex sentence** is similar to a compound sentence because it joins two clauses together, but complex sentences use subordinating conjunctions. We have already talked about using subordinating conjunctions as sentence starters, but you can also increase the complexity of your sentences by using them in the middle of sentences. Here are some examples:

Complex Sentences
Little vegetation can grow in the Sahara <u>because</u> it is so dry.
Einstein began working on his theory of gravity <u>after</u> he moved to Zurich .
You will succeed <u>if</u> you work hard.

In the above sentences, we have underlined each of the subordinating conjunctions. You can see that we have a clause both before and after that word. When you use a subordinating conjunction at the start of a sentence, you must put a comma between the two clauses. However, when the subordinating conjunction is in the middle of a sentence, as above, you do not use a comma at all.

Lastly, a **compound-complex sentence** contains elements of both kinds of sentences and will have a total of three clauses in it. Two of the clauses are joined by a coordinating conjunction, and one of those two clauses is joined to a third clause by a subordinating conjunction. Here are some examples:

Compound-Complex Sentences
While *<u>Albert Einstein worked</u> at the patent office, <u>he continued</u> developing his theories,* **and** *<u>he became</u> one of the world's most influential physicists.*
<u>Students</u> who use a planner <u>will be</u> better organized, **and** *<u>they are</u> less likely to forget important dates* **because** *<u>they can track</u> them on their calendar.*

In the above sentences, we have underlined the subject and verb of each clause and bolded the conjunctions. You can see that each sentence has three sets of subjects and verbs. This means that it contains three clauses. Each sentence also contains both a subordinating and coordinating conjunction in it.

Advanced Starters: Participial Phrases

We should note that there is another other quality sentence starter to use: the **participial phrase**. This one is more difficult, so do not feel you have to use it in your essays yet. However, it is important to understand it, because if you naturally use it in your essay, we want you to know that there is no need to change it to one of these other sentence starters. You may have learned about participles when learning to conjugate different verbs. The core parts of a verb are the past, present, past participle, and present participle. The past participle is the word used with the helping verb "had," while the present participle is the "-ing" form of the verb. Here are a few examples for you:

Verb	Past Participle	Present Participle
Study	*Studied*	*Studying*
Explore	*Explored*	*Exploring*
Teach	*Taught*	*Teaching*

A participial phrase is a group of words that begins with either the past or present participle, followed by an object that goes with it. The participial phrase always functions as an adjective. Here is a sentence that begins with a participial phrase:

Participial Phrase Starters	
Having emigrated to the United States in 1933, *<u>Einstein</u> <u>took</u> a position as Professor of Theoretical Physics at Princeton until he retired in 1945.*	*The subject of this sentence is "Einstein" and the verb is "took." "Having emigrated" is an adjective phrase describing Einstein.*

Because a participial phrase is an adjective, it will never be the subject of a sentence. This trait distinguishes a participial phrase starter from a subject sentence opener. "-Ing" words can also be used as nouns known as **gerunds**. Starting a sentence with a gerund is still using a subject sentence starter. Let's take a look at a few sentences to compare participial phrase starters to subject starters:

Sentences with Subject Starters
Studying for tests is essential to success.
Drawing a conclusion is the final step of the scientific method.

In the above sentences, "studying" and "drawing" are each the subject of a sentence, which means that they are not participial phrases. Again, we will not practice using these openers this year, but if you think you have inadvertently used one, ask your teacher if you have used it correctly. If you have, there is no need to change it.

Improving Your Ear for Rhythm

In the end, you can write an essay that uses all different sentences starters, varies the length of sentences, and never has more than two of the same openers in a row, but sometimes something is still missing. Another part of learning how to improve the structure your sentences comes from reading and memorizing well-structured sentences from famous speeches, poems, and essays. By reading these well-written compositions, you can develop both a better ear for rhythm and also learn what sounds best. In the appendix of this book, we have included some famous written works for you in order to practice identifying quality rhythms in the writing. Then, try reading your essay aloud and listen to the rhythm of your sentences.

Summary

The way you start your sentences and how many clauses they contain will determine how eloquent, interesting, and memorable your essay is. All sentences start with something (you can't have a sentence that "doesn't have" a sentence starter). Your job is to make sure you change them at least every few sentences in order to add variety to your writing. In addition, using a variety of simple, compound, complex, and compound-complex sentences will add to the fluency and rhythm of your writing.

Finally, always read your essays out loud (or even better, have someone read them to you) to see how your essay sounds. Hearing the sentences read aloud will help you spot choppy or repetitive sentence structures and ensure that each sentences flows smoothly. As we have discussed before, make every word count!

Reading Comprehension Questions

1. What are the different types of sentence starters? Which is the most common one that you should try to avoid?

2. How many of the same sentence starter can you have in a row before you should change it? How many different ones should you aim to have in each paragraph?

3. Besides sentence starters, what is the other way to vary the structure of your sentences?

4. Why will reading quality speeches and essays help improve your sentence structure?

ACTIVITY

Identifying Sentence Structure / Practice

Instructions: For each sentence below, write the type of sentence starter that it demonstrates and circle the type of sentence structure it has. All sentence are adapted from *Alice's Adventures in Wonderland* by Lewis Carroll.

Example: Presently, she began again.

Starter type: Adverb

Structure type: *Simple* (circled) *Compound* *Complex* *Compound-Complex*

1. When she got to the door, she found she had forgotten the little golden key.

Starter type: ______________________

Structure type: *Simple* *Compound* *Complex* *Compound-Complex*

2. At this moment, Alice felt a very curious sensation.

Starter type: ______________________

Structure type: *Simple* *Compound* *Complex* *Compound-Complex*

3. For instance, if you were inside, you might knock, and I could let you out.

Starter type: ______________________

Structure type: *Simple* *Compound* *Complex* *Compound-Complex*

4. If you knew Time as well as I do, you wouldn't talk about wasting it.

Starter type: ______________________

Structure type: *Simple* *Compound* *Complex* *Compound-Complex*

5. Suddenly, a footman in livery came running out of the wood.

Starter type: ______________________

Structure type: *Simple* *Compound* *Complex* *Compound-Complex*

ACTIVITY

Identifying Sentence Structure / Practice

Instructions: For each sentence below, write the type of sentence starter that it demonstrates and circle the type of sentence structure it has. All sentence are adapted from *Alice's Adventures in Wonderland* by Lewis Carroll.

6. There was a table set out under a tree in front of the house, and the March Hare and the Hatter were having tea at it.

Starter type: ______________________

Structure type: *Simple* *Compound* *Complex* *Compound-Complex*

7. When she got back to the Cheshire Cat, she was surprised to find quite a large crowd collected round it.

Starter type: ______________________

Structure type: *Simple* *Compound* *Complex* *Compound-Complex*

8. Alice had never been in a court of justice before, but she had read about them in books.

Starter type: ______________________

Structure type: *Simple* *Compound* *Complex* *Compound-Complex*

9. As soon as the jury had a little recovered from the shock of being upset, and their slates and pencils had been found and handed back to them, they set to work very diligently to write out a history of the accident.

Starter type: ______________________

Structure type: *Simple* *Compound* *Complex* *Compound-Complex*

10. Lastly, she pictured to herself how this same little sister of hers would, in the after-time, be herself a grown woman.

Starter type: ______________________

Structure type: *Simple* *Compound* *Complex* *Compound-Complex*

ACTIVITY

Revising Sentences / Practice

Instructions: Each sentence below uses a subject starter. Add more information and revise the sentence to create a sentence with each of the other starters indicated. You can rearrange, re-word, and add to the information in the sentence as long as it retains its meaning. See the example for further explanation.

Example: Perseverance is integral to success.

Prepositional phrase: Without perseverance, students cannot succeed.

Adverb: Certainly, perseverance is integral to success.

Subordinate conjunction: Because perseverance teaches students to never give up, it is integral to success.

Notice how each sentence retains the same meaning even though we changed the first sentence from positive to negative, and we added additional information to the third one.

1. Studying improves students' grades.

Prepositional Phrase: ____________________

____

Adverb: ____________________

Subordinate conjunction: ____________________

____

2. Water covers about 70% of the earth's surface.

Prepositional Phrase: ____________________

____

Adverb: ____________________

Subordinate conjunction: ____________________

____

ACTIVITY

Revising Sentences / Practice (Cont.)

Instructions: Each sentence below uses a subject starter. Add more information and revise the sentence to create a sentence with each of the other starters indicated. You can rearrange, re-word, and add to the information in the sentence as long as it retains its meaning. See the example for further explanation.

3. Students can improve their communication skills by working together in groups.

Prepositional Phrase: ______________________________

____

Adverb: ______________________________

Subordinate conjunction: ______________________________

____

4. People who practice self-reliance will improve their self-esteem.

Prepositional Phrase: ______________________________

____

Adverb: ______________________________

Subordinate conjunction: ______________________________

____

5. The alpine ibex is a type of goat that lives in the Alps and feeds on grass and shrubs.

Prepositional Phrase: ______________________________

____

Adverb: ______________________________

Subordinate conjunction: ______________________________

____

ACTIVITY

Combining Sentences / Practice

Instructions: For each question below, combine the simple sentences to form the type of sentence indicated using the provided conjunction. Make sure your finished sentence makes sense. See the example for more information.

Example: Students must first master grammar. Then, they proceed to logic. (Complex, "after")

After students master grammar, they proceed to logic.

Notice how we removed "first" and "then" because these words are no longer needed when they are combined using the subordinate conjunction "after." You could also answer this questions by saying, "Students proceed to logic <u>*after*</u> *they master grammar."*

1. Pandas eat for 12 hours a day. They only eat bamboo. (Complex, "since")

____

____

2. Knowledge of the fine arts is essential to a fulfilled life. It creates a more well-rounded person. (Complex, "because")

____

____

3. Reciting poetry helps improve your ear for rhythm. This recitation will help improve your writing. (Compound, "and")

____

____

4. Everyone can be a great writer. It takes practice. (Compound, "but")

____

____

ACTIVITY

Combining Sentences / Practice

Instructions: For each question below, combine the simple sentences to form the type of sentence indicated using the provided conjunction. Make sure your finished sentence makes sense.

5. You have a test coming up. Be sure to review your notes. You will do well. (Compound-Complex, "whenever" "and," ")

____

____

6. Studying is hard work. It is worth the effort. (Complex, "although")

____

____

7. You must always persevere. You want to succeed. (Complex, "if")

____

____

8. Things get difficult. Always keep trying. Don't be afraid to ask for help. (Compound-Complex, "when" "but,")

____

____

9. Take time to revise your essay carefully. You will strengthen your whole argument. (Compound, "and")

____

____

ESSAY

Journal Writing / Practice Makes Perfect

Write a fictional story beginning with the following sentence: ***"Oh, what have you done?" yelled my cousin as we ran for our lives.*** It can be funny, sad, or serious, but be sure to write neatly and with correct capitalization and punctuation. This journal entry is a chance for you to be creative. Do not worry about the sentence structure while you write, but when you are finished, go back and identify what kinds of sentences you ended up using naturally.

ESSAY

Essay

DIGITAL WATERCOLOR PAINTING OF PATH

Artwork by veneratio

Section IV
Writing for Different Purposes

CHAPTERS

THUNDERSTORM

Looking at this photo, you can almost smell the rain and hear the thunder. A well-written descriptive essay, like a magnificent photograph, should immerse the reader in the imagery, allowing them to actually experience what you describe.

Photo by freedom naruk

CHAPTER

Descriptive Writing

ROADMAP

- Understand the goal of descriptive writing.
- Analyze ways to make writing more descriptive.
- Distinguish between active and passive voice.
- Identify figures of speech to improve diction.
- Write a descriptive essay.

THALES OUTCOME

Nº 14

A person with **Gratitude** *acknowledges the gifts one has been given and the contributions of others.*

Recognizing the beauty in the world and being grateful for it is a necessary start to descriptive writing. Your appreciation for the beauty around you will shine through in your writing, making every word more vivid.

Descriptive Writing

THE GOAL OF A **descriptive essay** is to paint a picture for your reader. A well-written piece of descriptive writing allows your reader to visualize exactly what you describe. We will focus on three primary ways to improve your descriptive writing: word choice, sensory detail, and figures of speech.

Word Choice

Word choice may be the most important element in descriptive writing, so you should continue to practice what we discussed in Chapter 8 regarding improving your word choice. Focus on strong, active verbs, vivid adjectives, and engaging adverbs. It is especially important to avoid the "to be" verb because its forms (am, is, are, etc) introduce more words than are needed, preventing you from using stronger verbs.

Show don't tell

What sets apart a weak description from a strong one is whether you are "showing" us what is happening or "telling" us what is happening. One way to show rather than tell is by focusing on strong verbs, not just strong adjectives. If you have a quality adjective in mind, it can be tempting to use it as a **predicate adjective** with a linking verb instead of as an **attributive adjective** with an action verb. An attributive adjective comes directly before the noun it describes, while a predicate adjective follows after the noun it describes by using a linking verb. Perhaps you want to describe the flower in a meadow, and so you say, *The colors of the flowers are vibrant*. In this sentence, you have included a vivid adjective, *vibrant*, to describe *flowers*, but you have used it as a predicate adjective because it comes *after* the noun *flowers* and uses the linking verb *are*. A better way to write the sentence would be, *The vibrant flowers bloomed in the meadow*. Now we have used *vibrant* as an attributive adjective directly before the noun it describes (*flowers*), and instead of a linking verb, we have the action verb *bloomed*. Notice, though, to write the sentence properly, you must add more detail, usually through adding an action verb. Writing your sentence this way *shows* us more about the flowers rather than just *telling* us about them.

Active vs. Passive Voice

Another way "show" rather than "tell" is by using **active voice** sentences and avoiding **passive voice** sentences. Passive voice sentences often add an unnecessary "to be" verb and weaken the overall sentence. In an active voice sentence, the subject is doing the action of the verb. In a passive voice sentence, the subject is not doing the action of the verb; instead,

In a descriptive essay, the goal is to paint a vivid picture for your reader. Great writers accomplish this by using a vivid vocbulary that appeals to the senses, using active voice, and using various figures of speech.

Vocabulary

Descriptive Essay
An essay written to paint a clear picture for the reader.

Predicate Adjective
A descriptive word that follows a linking verb but describes the subject.

Attributive Adjective
A descriptive word that comes directly before the noun it describes.

Active Voice
A sentence in which the subject is doing the action of the verb.

Passive Voice
A sentence where the subject is receiving the action of the verb.

Sensory Detail
Information that triggers one of the five senses: taste, touch, sight, smell, and sound.

Figurative language
Using words in a way that goes beyond their literal dictionary definitions.

Simile
A figure of speech that compares two unrelated things using "like" or "as."

Metaphor
A figure of speech where one thing is stated to be another different thing.

Personification
Giving human traits to nonhuman objects or creatures.

Onomatopoeia
A word that represents and reflects a certain sound.

something is being done to the subject. It is receiving the action of the verb rather than performing it. Take a look at this chart of passive and active voice sentences:

Passive Voice	Active Voice
The flower petals were carried by the wind. *The action verb in this sentence is "carried" and the subject is "petals;" however, the petals were not carrying anything. It was the wind that did the action of carrying, so this sentence is in the passive voice.*	*The wind carried the flower petals across the meadow.* *The action verb in this sentence is still "carried" but now the subject is "wind." "Wind" did the action of the verb "carried," so this sentence is written in the active voice.*
The meadow is visited by thousands of birds each morning. *The action verb in this sentence is "visited" and the subject is "meadow;" however, "meadow" did not visit anything. It was "birds" that "visited," so this sentence is in the passive voice.*	*Thousands of birds visit the meadow each morning.* *The action verb in this sentence is "visit" but now the subject is "thousands" (of birds). These thousands of birds are doing the action of the verb, so this sentence is in the active voice.*

You can see that the sentences in the active voice paint a more engaging, vivid picture for the reader. Passive voice sentences are also unnecessarily wordy. Writing in the active voice almost always strengthens your writing.

Sensory Detail

Sensory detail refers to information that triggers one of the five senses: taste, touch, sight, smell, and sound. Appealing to these senses helps place the reader in the scene you are describing, allowing them to picture everything more clearly.

Often, we get so caught up in "sight" sense that we neglect the other, equally important senses. Not all the senses may be equally relevant to what you are describing, but try to appeal to three or four of the senses if the goal of your writing is to be as descriptive as possible.

Figurative language

Figurative language refers to using words in a way that goes beyond their literal dictionary definitions. We will discuss three types of figurative language in this chapter: similes and metaphors, personification, and onomatopoeia.

Similes and Metaphors

We discussed similes and metaphors in Chapter 4 when we learned about hooks, but it is also a way to improve the descriptive detail of your writing. To review, a simile uses the word "like" or "as" to compare two seemingly unrelated things. *The sun shown like a comforting friend* uses a simile. A metaphor is similar but it makes a comparison without the word "like" or "as." *The sun is a comforting friend* uses a metaphor. These compare the "sun" to a "friend," two very different things.

Sometimes a standard description does not fully capture the essence of something, or perhaps it states the details but does so in a bland, unfeeling fashion. Metaphors and similes help immerse the reader in the details. For example, perhaps you want to express how graceful Kristi Yamaguchi (a famous figure skater) skates. The sentence *Yamaguchi glides like a swan across the ice* presents us with an image rather than simply describing her skills.

Similes and metaphors can also provide a point of comparison. For example, many people cannot picture the enormity of an eagle's wingspan, so comparing it to another, more common item, can give the reader a clearer picture of its size. For example, stating, *The wandering albatross has a wingspan of three meters* does not convey the same effect as stating, *The wandering albatross's wingspan can reach as wide as four front doors!* This comparison gives particular strength to the image because we often see this width and can easily picture it.

It is important to note that a sentence can compare using "like" or "as" and not be a simile. If you were to say *Sarah is as tall as her sister* this would not be a simile because the sentence is comparing two similar things, two people. To be a simile or metaphor, you must be comparing two unalike things.

Personification

Personification refers to giving human traits to nonhuman objects or creatures, helping the reader feel the emotion in your words. We could say, *The boy was sad* or *The flowers were bright*, but using personification will add vibrancy to your writing. Perhaps *The boy's sad eyes welled with tears* or *The cheerful flowers brightened up the room*. Although a boy can be sad, eyes cannot be, and flowers cannot actually be cheerful. These are human characteristics, but applying them to the eyes or the flowers helps us feel the emotion of the sentence and visualize the images.

Onomatopoeia

Onomatopoeia refers to a word that represents and reflects a certain sound such as "squelch," "thud," or "purr." You can even create your own words by representing what you hear with letters. Bird watchers often describe sounds this way. While birds may "hoot" or "chirp," even more clear would be to say that they communicate with sounds of "kaw! kaw!" or "jay! jay! jay!" or "queedle-queedle."

Using onomatopoeia allows the reader to almost hear the sound as they read it. Instead of describing the sound, they could imagine hearing the actual sound.

Summary

In a descriptive essay, as in any essay, you need to craft paragraphs that use precise language. Focus on strong, vivid words that paint a picture for your readers and leave them feeling immersed in what you are describing. Be aware that although strong word choice is essential for all writing, descriptive writing can be more informal, so you would not use all these techniques in more formal research or scientific writing.

Active voice and sensory detail can improve all writing, but certain figures of speech, especially personification and onomatopoeia, would not be appropriate for very formal writing.

Reading Comprehension Questions

1. What is the goal of a descriptive essay?

2. What is the difference between predicate adjectives and attributive adjectives? Which is stronger? Why?

3. What is the difference between active and passive voice? Which voice is stronger? Why?

4. Which techniques from this chapter can you apply to formal writing? Which techniques should you avoid in formal writing?

ACTIVITY

Active vs. Passive Voice / Practice

Instructions: For each sentence below, identify whether it uses active or passive voice. If it is written in the passive voice, re-write it to be in the active voice. You can add additional information when re-writing the sentences. You may leave the line blank if the sentence is already in active voice. Sentences are adapted from *The Wonderful Wizard of Oz* by L. Frank Baum.

Example: The runners were chased by the dogs.

Active Voice (Passive Voice)

The dogs chased the runners.

1. The cellar was reached by a trap door in the middle of the floor.

Active Voice Passive Voice

____

2. Standing beside it, with an uplifted axe in his hands, was a man made entirely of tin.

Active Voice Passive Voice

____

3. He stood perfectly motionless, as if he could not stir at all.

Active Voice Passive Voice

____

4. She was moved by the sad voice in which the man spoke.

Active Voice Passive Voice

____

5. While they were walking through the forest, the Tin Woodman told the following story.

Active Voice Passive Voice

____

ACTIVITY

Avoiding Linking Verbs / Practice

Instructions: Re-write each of the sentences below so that it does not contain any "to be" verbs by using the underlined word as an attributive adjective or an action verb. You may need to add additional information to the sentence. Sentences are adapted from *The Wonderful Wizard of Oz* by L. Frank Baum.

Example: The Wicked Witch was both surprised and worried.

Surprised and worried by the girl's approach, the Wicked Witch called for her flying monkeys.

1. Dorothy oiled the tin man's neck, which was quite badly rusted.

2. If I roared very loudly, every living thing was frightened and got out of my way.

3. The lovely flowers became so thick that the ground was carpeted with them.

4. The girl was greatly astonished to find herself lying upon the grass.

5. The witch was angry to find them in her country.

6. The hats of the men were blue, and the little woman's hat was white.

ESSAY

Descriptive Essay / Assignment

Instructions: Write a 5-paragraph descriptive essay on one of the prompts below. Read all the guidelines carefully before beginning.

Length/Formatting Guidelines
• *Introduction and conclusion of at least three sentences each.* • *Three body paragraphs of at least four sentences (see topic choices for details).* • *Your essay should engage at least three of the senses.* • *Essay should have no more than five instances of the "to be" verb.* • *Essay should have at least two different types of figurative language* • *Essay should have a title, be double-spaced, and be free of major grammar/spelling issues.* *To review guidelines of what should be included in each paragraph, see appropriate chapters in this textbook and view the grading rubric on the next page.*

Topic Choices
1. *Choose an animal to write a descriptive essay about. Since this assignment is not a research essay, you should choose an animal that you frequently interact with so that you can regularly see it. This could be a common animal like a cardinal or a squirrel, or it could be a pet. Your three body paragraphs should describe what it looks like, what it sounds like (consider how it communicates or sounds it make while digging, eating, etc.), and what some of its common behaviors are.* 2. *Choose a favorite place you have. Be sure it is somewhere you have visited often so that you can describe it in detail. It could be a vacation spot, a grandparent's house, or any other place you frequent such as a library or café. You should choose three senses to focus on (taste, touch, sight, smell, or sound), and each body paragraph should focus on one sense.* 3. *Describe a beautiful scene in nature. It can be one you imagine or one that you have visited in real life. You should choose three senses to focus on (taste, touch, sight, smell, or sound), and each body paragraph should focus on one sense.*

Grading Rubric / Descriptive Essay after chapter 7

Below you will see the elements on which your essay will be graded. Details regarding each of these elements are outlined in the element's corresponding chapter.

Essay Component	*Criteria*	*Notes*
Formatting	Formatting ____/5	
Introduction	Hook ____/5 Thesis ____/5	
Organization	Structure of overall essay _____/5 Flow within paragraphs _____/10	
Evidence	Details in 1st body paragraph ______/5 Details in 2nd body paragraph ______/5 Details in 3rd body paragraph ______/5	
Descriptive Detail	Use of active voice _____/15 Use of sensory detail ______/20 Use of figurative language _____/10	
Conclusion	Summary ____/5 Clincher ____/5	

TOTAL: _______/100

APARTMENT BUILDING IN NEW YORK CITY

A bustling business district is founded on leaders and entrepeneurs with strong persuasive skills. They need to aquire loans, meet with clients, and continue to grow their business. The persuasive skills that you learn now will continue to help you for the rest of your life.

Painting by Ricardo Costa

CHAPTER

Persuasive Writing

ROADMAP

- Understand the goal of persuasive writing.
- Analyze ways to make writing more persuasive.
- Learn how to incorporate a rebuttal.
- Write a persuasive essay.

THALES OUTCOME

Nº 12

Traditional American Values *drives a leader to build and sustain a thriving economy.*

A leader and entrepreneur must possess effective skills of persuasion, which they use with integrity. Learning how to write a persuasive essay helps build the skills you need to convince others to recognize the strength of your reasons and impress upon them the importance of your ideas.

Writing the Persuasive Essay

THE GOAL OF A persuasive essay is to convince the reader to do or believe something. As we have talked about in past chapters, though, that does not mean that your essay should be written in the second person point of view. We will discuss four key considerations when attempting to be the most persuasive you can be: a strong thesis statement, quality word choice, effective evidence, and a rebuttal.

Thesis Statements

As we discussed in Chapter 2, a thesis statement is one to two sentences presenting your claim and your main points. When forming your thesis statement for a persuasive essay, make sure that it includes your point of view. In other words, you must state whether you are arguing for or against a particular idea. You cannot present the topic and give reasons both for and against it (that would be a compare-contrast essay). In a persuasive essay, you must be trying to convince your reader of something. If you were writing a persuasive essay about schools requiring dress code and you say, ***School dress codes promote professionalism, ease morning routines, and reduce bullying,*** you have created a thesis for an expository essay explaining how having a dress code does these things. It is not trying to convince the reader of a certain point of view. If you wanted to write a persuasive essay on this topic, you would need to establish what you are trying to convince you reader of, perhaps the idea that all schools ought to have dress codes. A good persuasive thesis statement could say, ***Schools should have dress codes because they promote professionalism, ease morning routines, and reduce bullying.*** Now you have an overall goal for regarding what you want your reader to believe.

Word Choice

As in any essay, word choice is important. The use of strong, active verbs will make your writing more persuasive. In addition, you want to be direct when attempting to persuade. More flowery language sets a more soothing tone while more direct, intense language sets a more powerful tone. Focusing on strong verbs will allow you to eliminate unnecessary adjectives and adverbs, which will make your writing more persuasive. Keep a thesaurus handy to help find stronger synonyms for your verbs. The end of this chapter also provides a chart listing many persuasive words.

Evidence

No matter your word choice, a good reader will be most swayed by your reasons in support of your claim and

In a persuasive essay, the goal is to convince the reader to do or believe something. This is done through having a strong thesis statement, using a precise vocabulary, and including high quality evidence.

Vocabulary

Persuasive Essay
An essay written to convince the reader to do or believe something.

Rebuttal
A paragraph in which the author addresses common counterarguments and attempts to refute them.

Counterargument
An argument against the original claim of the essay.

the evidence you provide to support those reasons. You can have a beautifully written essay, but if your evidence and explanations do not prove your claim, your reader will remain unconvinced. The best evidence is specific and objective. Your own opinions do not count as evidence. If you can do research, look for reliable sources with facts that support your points. If you are writing a persuasive essay without research, focus on personal experiences and facts you have learned from knowledgeable adults. Remember, after you present your evidence, you still need to analyze that evidence and explain how it applies to your main point.

Rebuttal

As you become a more accomplished writer, you can include a **rebuttal** in your persuasive essay. A rebuttal is a response to a **counterargument**, an argument against the main claim of your essay. Think of the common arguments against your thesis, and then see how you can explain either how those points are untrue or how they are less important than the reasons you presented. For example, a common argument against dress codes is that they are expensive. In a rebuttal, you could explain how you can find less expensive uniforms at Target, Walmart, or at used clothing stores. You can begin a rebuttal with a general topic sentence about common counterarguments such as, *Many people may argue that schools should not have dress codes because they can be very pricey.* Then you would give a few sentences rebutting (disproving) this: *However, many discount stores now sell uniform clothes. In addition, some schools host uniform exchanges, and many people resell their gently used uniforms.* Often, the rebuttal paragraph will come after your final body paragraph and before your conclusion. However, if your counterargument relates to only one of your main points, it is acceptable to put it after whichever body paragraph it applies to.

Hook & Clincher

The hook and clincher are often the hardest sentences to compose. For a hook in a persuasive essay, one strategy is to begin with a counterargument which your thesis will disprove, followed by your thesis statement. For example, a hook and thesis for a persuasive essay about dress codes could be, *School dress code can be frustrating for students, but their benefits far outweigh any annoyance. All schools should have dress codes because they promote professionalism, ease morning routines, and reduce bullying.* Because the thesis is a natural rebuttal to any counterargument, these sentences flow naturally from one to the next.

One effective clincher for a persuasive essay would be a "call to action." After all, you just spent multiple paragraphs convincing your reader to do or believe something. Your clincher is the perfect chance to tell them what to do next. Perhaps you may say *Support students by speaking to your school official*

Summary

In a persuasive essay, as in any essay, you need to craft eloquent paragraphs with strong evidence and effective language. Focus on strong, persuasive words that help set the tone for your essay and leave your reader feeling like they are reading something powerful and meaningful.

Word Choice / Persuasive Words

Strong verbs improve the persuasiveness of your writing. The chart below lists 85 persuasive verbs. You can use these as a starting point as you learn to improve your vocabulary. Feel free to add to this list when your come across other strong vocabulary words.

85 Persuasive Verbs				
Abolish	Connect	Illuminate	Inspire	Replace
Accelerate	Convert	Evaluate	Kindle	Resist
Achieve	Create	Evolve	Lead	Respond
Adopt	Define	Explore	Manage	Retain
Advance	Deliver	Extinguish	Master	Revolve
Advocate	Deploy	Finalize	Maximize	Simplify
Anticipate	Design	Focus	Motivate	Solve
Apply	Develop	Forge	Navigate	Succeed
Assess	Devour	Gain	Nurture	Supplement
Avoid	Diagnose	Gather	Overcome	Surge
Boost	Discover	Generate	Penetrate	Take
Bridge	Drive	Grapple	Persuade	Train
Build	Educate	Grasp	Prepare	Transfer
Capture	Eliminate	Identify	Prevent	Transform
Clarify	Ensure	Implement	Profit	Traverse
Comprehend	Establish	Improve	Propel	Unleash
Confront	Ignite	Increase	Reconsider	Yield

Reading Comprehension Questions

1. What is the goal of a persuasive essay?

2. What kind of words should you use to make your writing more persuasive?

3. What types of evidence are best for persuasive writing?

4. What is a rebuttal? Why does it make your writing more persuasive?

ESSAY

Persuasive Essay / Assignment

Instructions: You are writing a five-paragraph persuasive essay on one of the prompts below. You will support your thesis with two strong reasons as well as include a rebuttal paragraph addressing one or more common counterarguments.

Length/Formatting Guidelines

- *Introduction and conclusion of at least three sentences each.*
- *Two body paragraphs of at least four sentences that each contain one reason in support of your thesis.*
- *Third body paragraph of at least three sentences which presents a counterargument and provides a rebuttal for it.*
- *If typed, essay should be in MLA format.*
- *Essay should have a header, title, be double-spaced, and be free of major grammar/spelling issues.*
- *Essay should be revised for organization, word choice, and sentence structure.*

To review guidelines of what should be included in each paragraph, see appropriate chapters in this textbook and view the grading rubric on the next page.

Topic Choices

1. *People disagree on the benefits of homework. Do you think nightly homework has more benefits or harms? Pick one side to argue for. Be sure to support your essay with two strong reasons and a rebuttal paragraph refuting common counterarguments.*
2. *A standardized test refers to one that all students in a school or region take at the same time, with the same questions, under the same conditions. Tests like the IOWA, CLT, and the SAT are examples of standardized tests. Do you think required standardized testing in schools has more benefits or harms? Pick one side to argue for. Be sure to support your essay with two strong reasons and a rebuttal paragraph refuting common counterarguments.*
3. *P.E. stands for Physical Education. In some schools, students have P.E. every day, while at others, P.E. is only held once a week. In addition, many schools do not have their high school students take P.E. all 4 years. Do you think a physical education class should be required daily, or required regularly until graduation, or should P.E. be optional? Pick one side to argue for. Be sure to support your essay with two strong reasons and a rebuttal paragraph refuting common counterarguments.*
4. *Home economics is a class designed to teach practical home skills to students. Topics include things like cooking, sewing, and budgeting. Do you think a course like this should be required for students to take before graduation? Pick one side to argue for. Be sure to support your essay with two strong reasons and a rebuttal paragraph refuting common counterarguments.*

ESSAY

Grading Rubric / Persuasive Essay after Chapter 9

Below you will see the elements that you will be graded on. Details regarding each of these elements is outlined in its corresponding chapter.

Essay Component	*Criteria*	*Notes*
Formatting	Header ____/5 Formatting ____/5	
Introduction	Hook ____/5 Connecting sentence ____/5 Thesis ____/5	
Body Paragraph ***First Main Point***	Claim _____/5 Evidence/Analysis _____/5 Wrap-up _____/5	
Body Paragraph ***Second Main Point***	Claim _____/5 Evidence/Analysis _____/5 Wrap-up _____/5	
Rebuttal Paragraph	Statement of counterargument _____/5 Rebuttal to counterargument _____/5	
Conclusion	Summary ____/5 Clincher ____/5	
Overall Elements	Organization ____/5 Word Choice ____/10 Sentence Structure ____/10	

TOTAL: ______/100

ANCIENT AND MAGICAL LIBRARY

In this section we will learn how to gather research, create an outline, and ultimately write a research paper.

By Shaiith

Section V
Research Writing

CHAPTERS

BOOKS FOR SUCCESS

This book and light bulb represent the many ideas you will read about during the research process. You must be able to evaluate these ideas so that you can cull the weak, using only strongest, most reliable evidence to strengthen your argument.

Image by Surasak

CHAPTER

The Research Process

ROADMAP

- Learn how to use key terms to find information.
- Evaluate the reliability of sources.
- Identify best practices when taking notes from sources.
- Practice taking research notes.

THALES OUTCOME
Nº 7

Competent Technical Skills *allow individuals to join modern technological industries and navigate modern life.*

Competent technical skills are essential in the research process. You will need to know how to navigate electronic sources, find information, and organize that information.

The Research Process

WE HAVE LEARNED how to write and revise basic essays, but we have not yet learned how to research concepts or incorporate that research into an essay. **Research** refers to the process of investigating and learning more about a topic through books, lectures, videos, and journals. It is a skill like any other. You must learn how to search for sources, how to evaluate them, how to incorporate them into the body of your essay, and how to cite them. In this chapter, we will focus on how to find and evaluate sources.

Print Sources

A **print source** refer to an item found in a physical print format. Books, encyclopedias, magazines, and newspapers are all items you can find in a physical form. As our world becomes more technologically focused, we must remember that we can still research and find information in print sources. These sources have an advantage over electronic sources in that they are often (though not always) more well-researched and their information more reliable. As we will discuss shortly, anyone can put something on the internet, so we need to follow a strict process to evaluate online sources before we trust them.

When researching a topic, you can go to your local library or even a book store to find books, journals, and magazines to read. However, be careful of **tabloids**. Tabloids, often found at grocery store checkout aisles, look like magazines or newspapers, but often capture people's attention with sensational headlines. They are notorious for containing inaccurate or exaggerated information or information taken out of context. You also need to be careful with newspapers, although some newspapers are more reliable than others. When reading magazines and newspapers for your research, compare them with other sources to verify that the facts you have found are accurate.

Electronic Sources

Let us move into using search engines to find information. A **search engine** is a program into which you type key terms and receive back internet results related to those terms. Currently, the most popular search engine is Google. When you navigate to Google's website at *www.google.com*, you can type in key words to find articles for your research. You must choose your search terms carefully. For example, imagine your topic is "Who was Hadrian, and why do you think he was considered one of the 'five good emperors'?"

The research process, though often arduous and time consuming, is the foundation of a quality research paper. You must take time to carefully evaluate any source you plan to use to ensure that your information is accurate and reliable.

Vocabulary

Research
The process of investigating and learning more about a topic through books, lectures, videos, and journals.

Print Source
An item found in physical print format.

Tabloids
Magazines or newspapers that capture people's attention with sensational headlines and are notorious for containing inaccurate or exaggerated information or information taken out of context.

Search Engine
A program into which you type key terms and receive back internet results related to those terms.

Research Databases
Searchable collections of information online, especially journal articles.

Peer-reviewed
An article that has been checked by experts to verify its facts and quality.

When we type "Hadrian" into the Google search engine, this is what we get as our first five results. Of these five, only one is a usable source. Let's take a look:

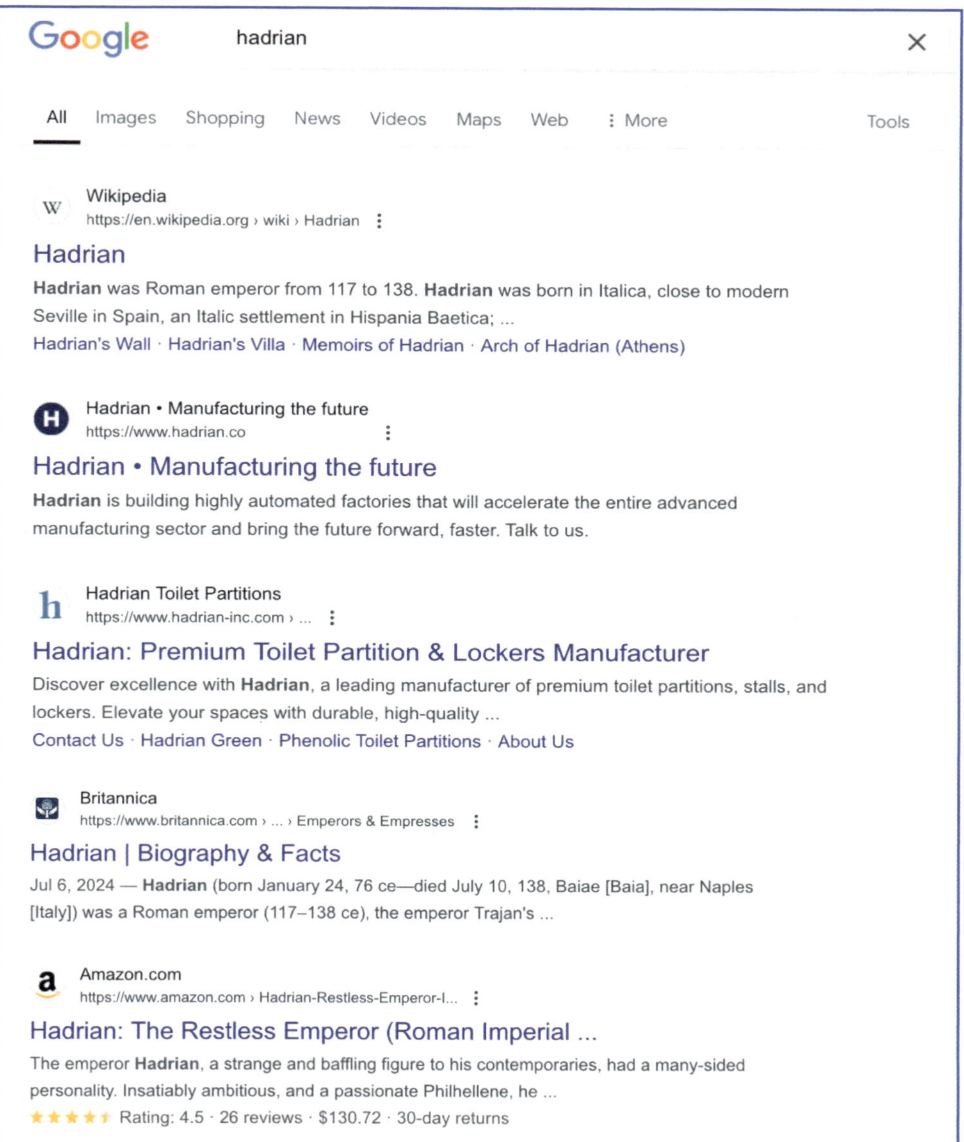

Our first result is an article from Wikipedia. Wikipedia is an unreliable source and should not be used for research. We will discuss evaluating sources shortly. Our second result is a manufacturing company—probably not the Hadrian we are looking for. Our third result is also not related to the ancient Roman named Hadrian; it's a website for a company that makes partitions and lockers for restrooms. Our fourth result finally gives us a good source: Britannica, a respected encyclopedia.

Lastly, our fifth result is for a product on Amazon—also not useful unless you plan to purchase and read a book about Hadrian.

You can see from these results that only typing "Hadrian" into the search was not specific enough to get many quality sources on our topic. If you try adding one or two other key words, you will get more precise results. If you search for "Hadrian Roman emperor" you get a plethora of articles about the Roman emperor Hadrian as you can see below:

To be clear, Google is not a source, it is merely a tool to help you find sources. You should not cite from the search engine screen. You must click on one of the results, which would be your source.

Now, you don't want to get too specific in your search for two reasons: one, you want to make sure that you

12:41 PM Tue Aug 20

hadrian roman emperor

hadrian roman emperor

English Heritage
https://www.english-heritage.org.uk › visit › hadrians-wall

Emperor Hadrian

Publius Aelius Hadrianus (AD 76–138), known to us as **Hadrian**, was born in **Rome** on 24 January AD 76. His family – the Aelii – were from Italica in the **Roman** ...

Amazon.com
https://www.amazon.com › Hadrian-Restless-Emperor-I...

Hadrian: The Restless Emperor (Roman Imperial ...

The **emperor Hadrian**, a strange and baffling figure to his contemporaries, had a many-sided personality. Insatiably ambitious, and a passionate Philhellene, he ...

★★★★½ Rating: 4.5 · 26 reviews · $130.72 · 30-day returns

Ancient Rome Live
https://ancientromelive.org › hadrian

People & Personalities | Emperor Hadrian

Hadrian ruled as **Roman emperor** from 117 to 138 CE. Learn about him, his history, and his impact on the city of Rome here.

World History Encyclopedia
https://www.worldhistory.org › hadrian

Hadrian

May 18, 2021 — **Hadrian** (l. 78-138 CE) was **emperor** of **Rome** (r. 117-138 CE) and is recognized as the third of the Five Good **Emperors** (Nerva, Trajan, **Hadrian**, ...

find enough information; and two, you need to make sure you are still writing your own paper, which you support with research, not relying on the articles to come up with your ideas for you. For instance, you should not be searching "Was Hadrian a good emperor?" It is up to you to research the life of Hadrian and then explain yourself whether he was good. Try searches like "Hadrian Roman accomplishments" and you will find articles specifically geared towards what he did in his life. Then, you will read and take notes before forming your ideas, which we will discuss later.

Online Library Resources

Besides Google, you can also visit your local library's website. The library is not just a physical location to borrow books from; they also usually have sections on their website specifically dedicated to research. If you navigate to the website of the Wake County (NC) Public Library, you will see an option for "Research" which takes you to the screen you see at the bottom of this page.

These are paid resources that you can access for free with that region's library card. The main category that will be useful to your research are research databases. **Research databases** are searchable collections of information, especially journal articles. Now, we don't mean a journal like what you might use to record personal reflections. An academic journal is like a magazine focused on one profession or industry. The articles are written by professionals in their field and contain well-researched information. One particular database that you will use as you get into more advanced areas of study is called JSTOR. This is a paid database to which some institutions maintain a monthly subscription. For more information or to find out if your school subscribes to JSTOR, speak with your teacher.

Evaluating Sources

In today's day and age, electronic sources are abundant and easy to access. You have more access to information than any generation before you. However, it

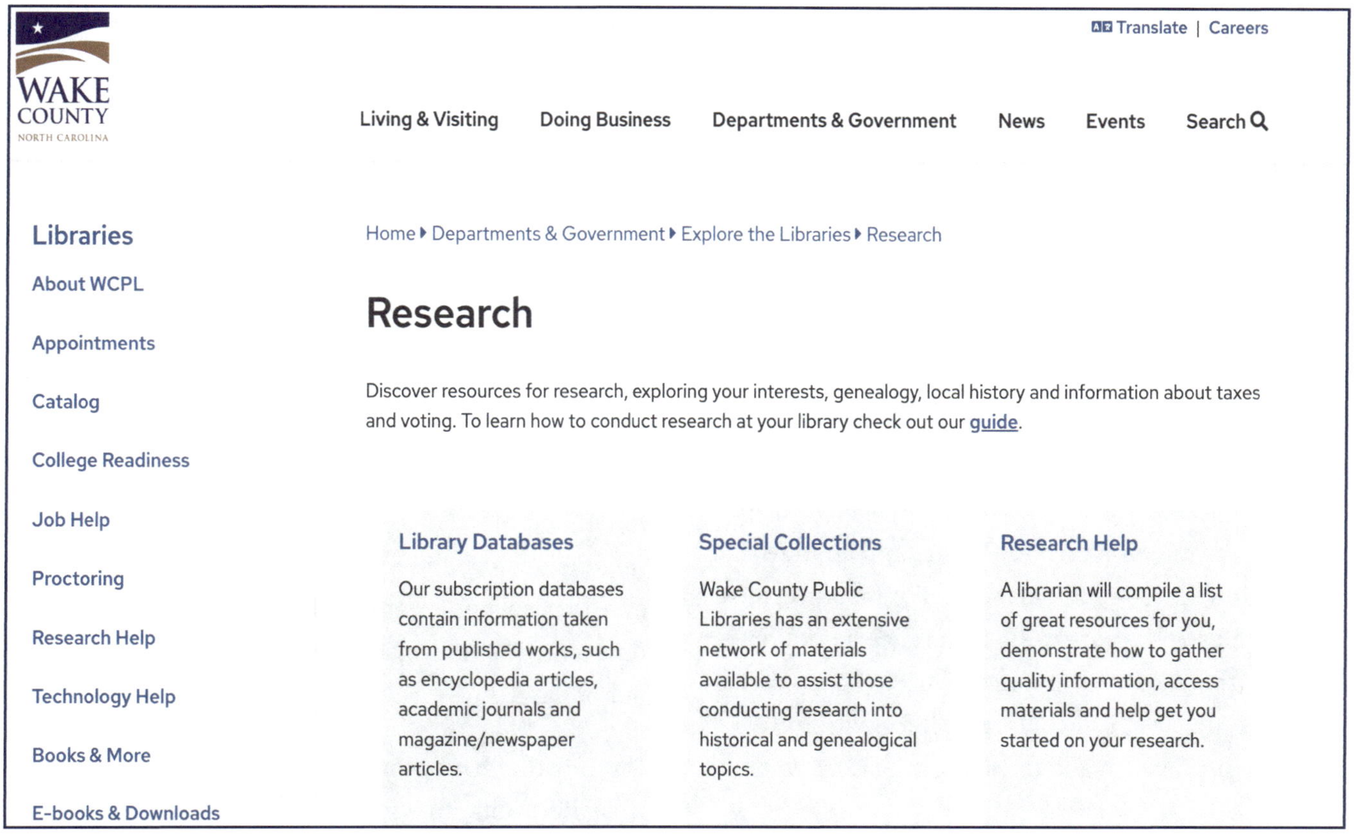

WAKE COUNTY
NORTH CAROLINA

Translate | Careers

Living & Visiting   Doing Business   Departments & Government   News   Events   Search

Libraries
About WCPL
Appointments
Catalog
College Readiness
Job Help
Proctoring
Research Help
Technology Help
Books & More
E-books & Downloads

Home ▸ Departments & Government ▸ Explore the Libraries ▸ Research

Research

Discover resources for research, exploring your interests, genealogy, local history and information about taxes and voting. To learn how to conduct research at your library check out our guide.

Library Databases
Our subscription databases contain information taken from published works, such as encyclopedia articles, academic journals and magazine/newspaper articles.

Special Collections
Wake County Public Libraries has an extensive network of materials available to assist those conducting research into historical and genealogical topics.

Research Help
A librarian will compile a list of great resources for you, demonstrate how to gather quality information, access materials and help get you started on your research.

is not enough to find the information, you now have to evaluate the reliability and accuracy of that information. Even from a phone, you can access articles from scientific journals that previously could only be found in large university research libraries. (What a triumph of modern technology!) But you can also find 16-year-old Jimmy's website that he created to prank his sister into believing that unicorns are real.

Given all the information we can find online, how do we filter the good from the bad? There are five different areas you should consider: ***authority***, ***objectivity***, ***currency***, ***accuracy***, and ***appearance***

Authority

To determine if the information you found is credible, first determine who wrote the article, and then analyze his or her credentials. Often, you can click on the author's name to view his or her biography. Read through the provided biography to see if they are a reliable source of information. Consider the following questions:

- What is their education? Did they receive a degree in this particular field?
- What is their experience? Even if they don't have a degree in this field, have they gained enough first-hand experience to be knowledgeable in this area?
- Are they biased? Do they have a particular motive to sway you in one direction or another?

Some articles will not list an author or they will say "Staff Writer" or "Editors." If a specific person's name does not appear as the author, then you need to determine who created or manages the site and analyze that organization for reliability and bias. For instance, most of the articles on Encyclopedia Britannica do not have specific authors, but the organization is respected and strives to only post verified, factual information. To find more information about the organization, go to the "About" section and read about the organization, considering the following questions:

- Is this organization biased? Does it have a particular motive to sway you in one direction or another?
- Where are they getting their information from?
- Are they a reputable organization?

Objectivity

Objectivity refers to whether the author or the website has any biases. It is important that the articles you read contain objective information—they do not try to sway you towards one opinion or another. A biased source favors a particular point of view and attempts to persuade its audience in one direction. For instance, information about animal testing from PETA (People for the Ethical Treatment of Animals) may not be as reliable as an article from a scholarly journal from *Advanced Science*. That's not to say that the information on a website with certain points of view are automatically false. Rather, you should read unbiased, scholarly articles for your research rather than relying on possibly biased information. A biased source may take information out of context or not tell you the full story.

Currency

How recently the article was written may be relevant to its reliability. If you are writing about the effects of technology on children, then you should make sure your information is recent. If the article is from the 1990s, the facts present may not apply to your argument. Before society was saturated with smartphones, text messaging, and various social media websites, the effects of technology on children would have been different. The information in that article is probably out of date.

On the other hand, some topics change very little over time. Returning to our Hadrian example, you can find plenty of older articles that will still contain accurate information. Remain vigilant, though. Perhaps new discoveries were made or additional information was discovered that may affect what we know about him.

In order to verify the currency of an article, look for a date. Often these dates appear at the beginning of an article, near the author's name. You may also look for a copyright date at the very bottom of the screen to verify the currency of the information.

Accuracy

If you are otherwise unfamiliar with the subject matter, it is important to verify the facts by reading articles from more than one source. If only one article provides the information you found, the information may be inaccurate, exaggerated, or taken out of context.

An article that is **peer-reviewed** has been checked by experts to verify the facts and quality of the article. Journal articles from databases like JSTOR are often peer-reviewed.

Appearance

Another way to evaluate a website is to examine its appearance. A website which is poorly formatted, disorganized, or full of pop-up ads is probably not a reliable source. A well-established organization will not usually need to rely on the income of ads and pop-ups, and a poorly formatted website implies that they are not a reputable organization.

Questions to Ask

Here are some questions you should ask about every source to ensure it is reliable and meets all the standards we have mentioned:

- Who created the site or wrote the article? Is the organization/person credible and an expert in this field?
- When was the article published or the website last updated? Consider whether the information is still up-to-date.
- What is the domain? For example, is it a *.org* site (more reliable) or a *.com* site (often less reliable).
- Does the layout and format present the information in a professional manner?
- Is there any evidence of bias (favoring a certain point of view) on the site?

Below are some websites you will encounter frequently in your research that you should always avoid:

Websites to Avoid	
Wikipedia	*This website can be edited by anyone and therefore may contain inaccurate information. However, take a look at the citations at the bottom of the article and you may find some reliable sources to go to directly.*
Blogs	*These are people's personal websites and should not be used for research.*
Question/ Answer Sites	*These can be posted or answered by anyone and are not a reliable source of information.*
Generic information websites	*These websites, like study.com, give broad facts but do not provide expertly-written, detailed information.*
Tabloids/ Sensational websites	*These look like magazines or newspapers, but often capture people's attention with sensational headlines and are notorious for containing inaccurate or exaggerated information or information taken out of context.*
Opinion articles	*Newspapers can be a reliable source of information, but make sure you avoid articles housed in the "Opinion" section, unless you need them. These are simply someone's opinion and may not have verified facts to back them up.*

Taking notes

Once you have found a reliable source, it is time to take notes. First, be sure that you put the link or citation information at the top of your notes. You will need to know where each fact came from to be able to cite your sources when including this information in your essay. (We will discuss how to cite sources in a future chapter.) When you proceed to a new article, record the citation information for that new source before writing your notes below it.

When you take your notes, don't write down entire sentences. Instead, use bullet points to record key information. Bullet points will help you put the facts into your own words when it is time to write your essay and ensure that you do not plagiarize.

Below is a sample of what your notes should look like. Notice that you always include a header and title at the top of your paper. Then, include the link or book title so you remember which source each fact came from. Finally, below each source, take your notes in bulleted, keyword form.

Ben Franklin
Grammar
Mr. Socrates
10/25/24

Research Notes on Kiwi Bird

Source: Smithsonian's National Zoo and Conservation Biology Institute
https://nationalzoo.si.edu/animals/north-island-brown-kiwi

- Flightless
- 1.5-2ft tall
- From New Zealand
- Eats earthworms, beetles, snails, crayfish, insects, and fruits
- Nocturnal

Source: Encyclopedia Britannica
https://www.britannica.com/animal/kiwi-bird

- 5 different species
- Nostrils at tip of beak
- Hairlike feathers
- Sleeps in forests

Reading Comprehension Questions

1. What should you keep in mind when choosing key words to use in an internet search?

2. Besides using a search engine like Google, where else can you go for information when researching?

3. Explain what Wikipedia is and why it is not a reliable source of information. What can you learn from a Wikipedia article?

4. Explain what a tabloid is and why it is not a reliable source of information.

ACTIVITY

Finding Reliable Sources / Research Activity

Instructions: For each of the following topics, find a reliable article, write down a few notes with facts you learned, and explain how you know the article is credible/reliable.

Topic	Resource Used	Notes	Explanation of credibility
The Fall of Rome			
The Printing Press			
The Moon Landing			
Italian Sculptor Michelangelo			

ACTIVITY

Finding Reliable Sources / Research Activity

Instructions: For each of the following topics, find a reliable article, write down a few notes with facts you learned, and explain how you know the article is credible/reliable.

Mozart's Childhood			
Benefits of Learning a Foreign Language			
The Pythagorean Theorem			
The Bill of Rights			

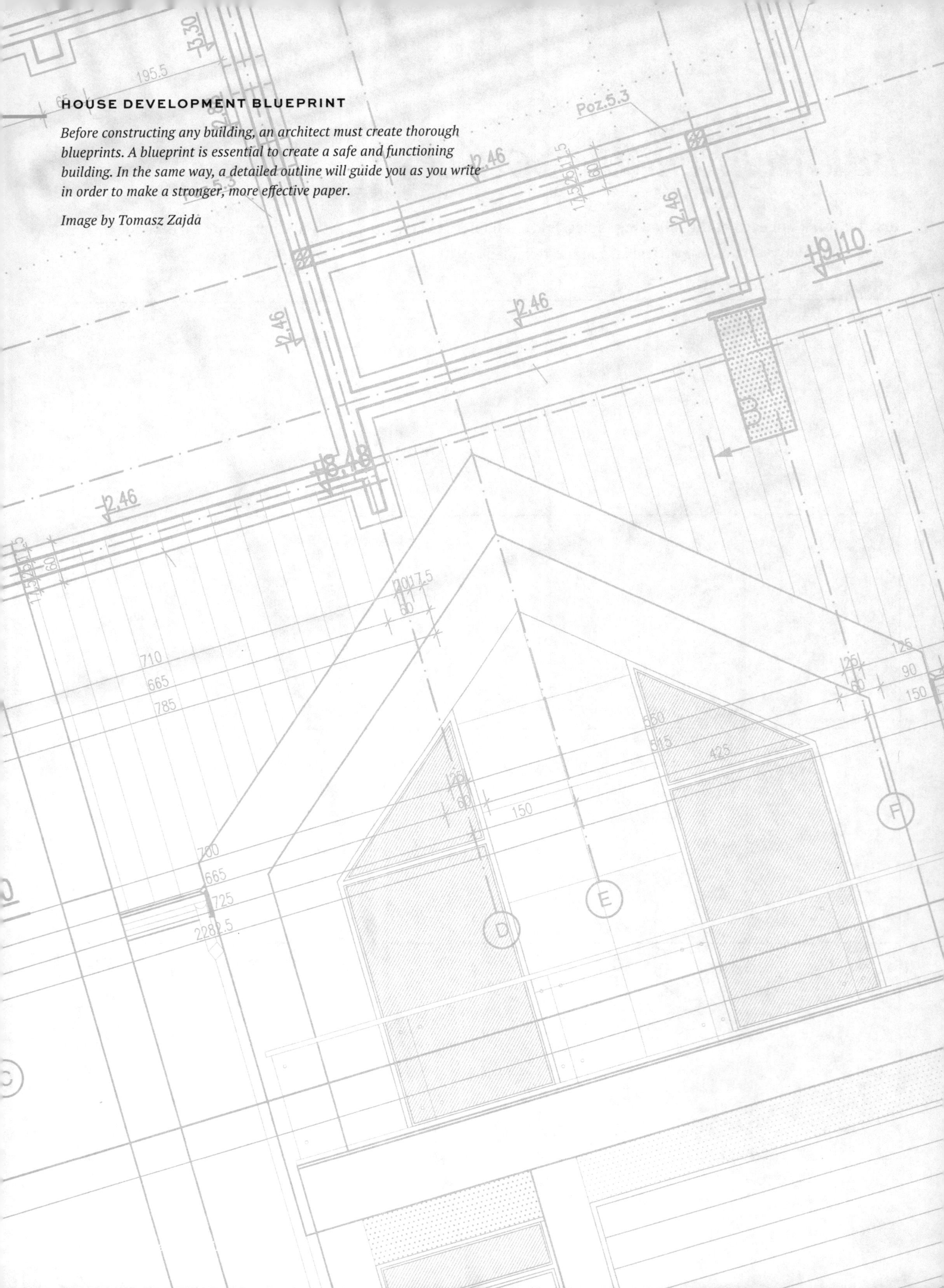

HOUSE DEVELOPMENT BLUEPRINT

Before constructing any building, an architect must create thorough blueprints. A blueprint is essential to create a safe and functioning building. In the same way, a detailed outline will guide you as you write in order to make a stronger, more effective paper.

Image by Tomasz Zajda

CHAPTER 13

Outlining

ROADMAP

- Understand how to create alphanumeric outlines.
- Learn how to incorporate research into your outline.
- Practice creating key word outlines.

THALES OUTCOME

Nº 4

A **Truth Seeker** *searches for the correct, right, or accurate explanation of reality.*

Your outline is a chance organize all the information you have found. You will often find, as you do so, that even more research is needed to support some of your points. The pursuit of truth will enable you to create the best outline and essay possible.

Organizing and Outlining

IN THE LAST CHAPTER we discussed the first step of the research process: taking notes. Once you have taken plenty of notes, it is time to organize your notes and create an outline.

First, group your notes into main ideas. If you were researching a Roman leader, for instance, you might have notes on his childhood, education, accomplishments, popularity (or lack thereof), and death. A good method for grouping your notes is to use different colored highlighters for each category and highlight each fact in your notes accordingly. This way, your notes are still grouped according to which source they came from. If you choose to re-write your notes while grouping them into categories, be sure that you indicate which source each fact came from.

Now that you have categorized your notes, decide what the main points of your essay will be. Perhaps you will focus on your leader's childhood, political life, and downfall. On the other hand, maybe you decide to focus on the leader's education, political accomplishments, and philanthropic endeavors. What you choose to focus on depends on the prompt you are responding to and the argument you want to make.

Outlining

After you have categorized your notes and chosen your main points, you are ready to create an **outline**. An outline lists your main points along with subpoints and specific information that you plan to include in your essay. A detailed outline provides the foundation for a strong essay. A quality outline will help you organize your ideas and see how your ideas fit together and flow from one to the next, as well as ensuring that you have an adequate amount of relevant evidence to prove your points.

An outline is like a more detailed essay map. Like an essay map, your outline is organized into main points, but each main point is divided into a variety of subpoints and sub-subpoints that provide further details of your planned essay. Essay maps are simpler outlines that work well for shorter essays, but a research essay calls for a more detailed outline.

Outlines come in many forms: sentence outlines, key word outlines, alphanumeric outlines, and bullet outlines. In this chapter we will focus on the traditional **alphanumeric outline.** An alphanumeric outline provides a clear map for each paragraph of an essay by

Every outline, like every essay, is different and unique. It is up to you to decide how you support your argument and organize your points so that your paper flows naturally and logically from beginning to end.

Vocabulary

Outline
A document that provides a clear map of each paragraph in an essay by listing the key information under various letters and numbers to show how the points and evidence will be arranged in the essay.

Alphanumeric Outline
A type of outline that lists the key information under various letters and numbers to show how the points and evidence will be arranged.

Parallel Language
Using the same part of speech and structure for each item, phrase, or clause in a list.

listing the key information under various letters and numbers to show how the points and evidence will be arranged.

Every Outline is Different

First of all, you must understand that all outlines are different. Repeat that. All outlines are different. A five-paragraph essay is often seen as the standard essay format. In this case your outline would have three main points, each of which is supported in its own paragraph, along with an introduction or conclusion. But perhaps you have four main points you would like to discuss. Or perhaps you would like to include a rebuttal after your main points. Your teacher can give you more guidance on how many points a particular essay should include.

Even if you and all your peers are required to have the same number of main points, each one of your main points can include any number of subpoints and often sub-subpoints (or even sub-sub-subpoints!). Again, every outline is different. For example, you can see below how two students might create two different outlines for a paragraph about the same topic:

Student 1 Outline	Student 2 Outline
II. Studying	*II. Studying*
A. Frequency	*A. Tests*
1. 15 minutes per class	*1. Study guides*
2. Nightly	*a. Get correct answers*
B. Environment	*b. Recreate to practice*
1. Uninterrupted	*2. Notes*
2. Quiet	*B. Homework*
3. Comfortable	*1. Every day*
	1. Review notes
	2. Write down questions
	2. Distraction-free environment

You can see how each main point ("studying" in this case) can have a variety of subpoints and how each student uses different wording, even when their ideas are the same.

Those were both samples of the alphanumeric outline, the most traditional style of outline. This style of outline is distinguished by Roman numerals, capital and lowercase letters, and Arabic numerals. Outlines can be written in key words or complete sentences. Below is the general structure of an alphanumeric outline:

Structure of an outline

I. Introduction
- A. Hook
- B. Background Information
- C. Thesis

II. First Main point
- A. Supporting idea
    - 1. Example/Evidence
        - a. Additional information as needed
        - b. Additional information
- B. Supporting idea
    - 1. Example/Evidence
    - 2. Example/Evidence

III. 2nd Main point
- A. Supporting idea
    - 1. Example/Evidence
        - a. Additional information as needed
        - b. Additional information
    - 2. Example/Evidence

The main point level uses Roman numerals (I, II, III, etc), the supporting idea or subpoint level uses capital letters (A, B, C, etc), the evidence level uses Arabic numerals (1, 2, 3, etc), and the additional information level uses lowercase letter (a, b, c, etc). You can technically continue to subdivide points as needed, but four levels should be sufficient for most outlines you will be writing in middle school.

As you can see in the sample structure, each level is progressively indented more and more, but each type of level line up throughout the whole outline. In other words, Roman numerals all line up, lower case letters all line up, and so forth.

Points and Subpoints

To create an alphanumeric outline, you need to know the proper numbers and letters to use. The main points will be your broadest category, which you represent with capitalized Roman numerals (I, II, III, IV, etc). For shorter essays, like the ones you will write in middle school, each Roman numeral usually corresponds with a paragraph. In high school, when you begin to write much longer essays, you might have three main points labeled with your Roman numerals, but in your essay, those points will be broken down into multiple paragraphs.

Beneath each Roman numeral, you will have subpoints represented by capital letters (A, B, C, etc.). These divide the main point into the different elements you plan to write about. For instance, if your first paragraph is about a person's childhood, your subpoints might be "Birth" and "Family," or "Birth," "Family," and "Education."

Now, each main point will always have a few capital letter subpoints beneath it, but there may also be sub-subpoints represented by Arabic numerals (1, 2, 3, 4, etc). These allow you to go into more detail about your subpoints. These sub-subpoints can even have lowercase letters under them to go into even more depth.

Here is a sample to show you what these different letters and numbers look like:

Using Numbers and Letters in an Outline
II. Herbivores
A. Frugivores
1. Fruit-eaters
2. Examples
a. Bats
b. Flying foxes
B. Folivores
1. Leaf-eaters
2. Examples
a. Koalas
b. Pandas
c. Asian elephant
III. Carnivores

Although the above outline is unfinished, we can examine its structure. That way you can better understand how to make your own outline. In this partial outline, there are two main points: "Herbivores" and "Carnivores." The first main point has been divided into two subpoints: "Frugivores" and "Folivores." Then beneath each of those, there is a definition and list of examples. You can see how after you write subpoints for a particular main point, you can then return to create an additional main point which is then broken down into its own subpoints.

Parallel Language

When we create key word outlines, we should use parallel language. We discussed parallel language in Chapter 2 when discussing thesis statements, but let's review what it means.

Parallel language refers to using the same part of speech and structure to begin each item in a list. For example, items in a list might all be nouns, verbs ending in "-ing," or adjectives. Each item within the same list should match the format of all the other items in that list. In the same way, all items within the same level in an outline should use parallel language. If you were creating an outline about your favorite sports, it would be incorrect to list "to ski," "running," and "skate." This list is not written in parallel language because each of these is a different part of speech. Instead, you could list them as "skiing," "running," and "skating." Let's look at a correct and incorrect example.

Correct Use of Parallel Language	
II. Studying A. Frequency B. Environment III. Managing your time A. Using a calendar B. Looking ahead	*In this outline, items of the same level in the same section are all parallel. Roman numeral I and II are both "-ing" verbs.* *Under "studying," our subpoints are both nouns. Under "managing your time" our subpoints are both -ing verbs. Notice that the subpoints of II do not need to match the subpoints of III.*

Not in Parallel Language	
II. Studying A. Tests B. Homework III. Time management A. Calendar B. Plan ahead	*In this outline, items of the same level are not parallel. Roman numeral II is an "-ing" verb, but Roman numeral III is a noun.* *A and B under II are parallel because they are both nouns, but A and B under III are not parallel. "Calendar" is a noun and "Plan ahead" is a verb phrase.*

Incorporating Research

If you are creating an outline for a research paper, you must continue to keep track of which source your information came from. Whenever you add a fact from your research, be sure you indicate the author, title of the work, or some other key piece of information. That way, you can properly cite this information when you write your essay.

In addition, as you work on turning your notes into an outline, you may find that you do not have enough information. Perhaps you chose "Childhood" as one of your main points, but you only have a location and the date the person was born. You will need to conduct additional research in order to have enough information to write a paragraph about that main point. In this instance, perhaps you research the person's family, childhood home, or early education and add those details to your outline. As before, be sure to keep track of the source for each fact so that you can properly cite them, which we will discuss in the next chapter.

Words to Avoid

Outlines should not have words like "Why" or "How" unless you have subpoints underneath it to answer or explain the question. Your outline needs to have the facts, details, and explanations you plan to include in your essay, not a statement that you are going to explain them. Ultimately, a well-written outline will have everything you need to write your essay. If your outline says things like, "When he was born" but does not give the actual date, you won't be able to use that outline to actually write your essay.

In the same way, outlines should not have words like "analyze" or "explain" unless you have subpoints underneath it analyzing or explaining it. The outline should actually take you longer to write than the rough draft, because you must include all the facts and ideas. When it is time to write your rough draft, all you have to do is turn those key words into sentences.

Capitalization and Punctuation

In an outline, the number or letter at the start of a line should always have a period after it. In addition, the start of each line should always be capitalized. Do not treat all the information on a line like a title, though. You only capitalize the first word unless you have words that need to be capitalized for some other reason. Here is another outline example so you can see what this looks like:

Correctly Formatted	Explanation
II. Jane Austen's childhood A. Born in 1775. B. Grew up in the country III. Jane Austen's books A. *Emma* B. *Pride and Prejudice* C. *Northanger Abbey* D. *Sense and Sensibility*	*Notice how the first letter of each line is capitalized no matter what. Other words may be capitalized, but only if it's normally capitalized outside of an outline. "Austen" is her last name, and the main words in book titles are always capitalized.*

Using Word Processing Software to Help You

Word processing software like Google Docs, Apple Pages, and Microsoft Word can help you format your outline. Once you have given your document a header and title, select the bullets and numbering feature. Choose one that shows the same letters and numbers for each level that we have been discussing. That should cause a Roman numeral I to appear. Then, type your first main point and click "enter" or "return" to go to the next line. This will cause a Roman numeral II to appear. If you want to create a subpoint, click the increase indent button or tab key, and the line will move to the right and the Roman number II will change to letter A. If you have finished all your subpoints under a certain header, then you can click the decrease indent button and it will move left and revert to the previous level's number or letter.

All in all, learning to write outlines takes hard work and dedication. You must keep remember to number, indent, capitalize, and punctuate correctly, in addition to including quality information.

Reading Comprehension Questions

1. Why should you create an outline before writing an essay?

2. How should you indent in an outline? Why should you indent this way?

3. How should you capitalize and punctuate the items in an outline?

4. What does the term "levels" refer to in an outline?

ACTIVITY

Creating Outlines / Practice

Instructions: Practicing outlining an already-written paragraph can help you learn how to properly structure your own outline. Use the paragraph below to fill in the outline. Some of the information has already been filled in to help you get started.

1. Exercise is good for cardiovascular health. When people exercise and get their body moving, their heart beats faster to pump more blood. Because the heart is a muscle, exercise helps it grow stronger just like other muscles. Exercise also helps control blood pressure. Exercises like riding bikes, skating, and running keep blood flowing well. Heart health is just one of many reasons to exercise regularly.

I. ____________________

A. Heart muscle

1. ____________________

2. ____________________

3. ____________________

B. Lower blood pressure

C. ____________________

1. ____________________

2. Skating

3. ____________________

ACTIVITY

Creating Outlines / Practice

Instructions: Practicing outlining an already-written paragraph can help you learn how to properly structure your own outline. Use the paragraph below to fill in the outline. Some of the information has already been filled in to help you get started.

1. Finding an effective study spot is key to a successful school year. First, quality study spots should be free of distractions. Students should establish their study space away from the main living area where they may be distracted by siblings, pets, and televisions. They should also leave any phones or other devices in a separate room. Secondly, the study space should be comfortable, but not too comfortable. In particular, students should sit in a supportive chair at a desk or table. This seating arrangement keeps them engaged and ultimately leads to more effective studying.

I. ______________________________

A. ______________________________

1. ______________________________

2. No pets

3. ______________________________

4. ______________________________

B. ______________________________

1. ______________________________

2. Desk or table

ACTIVITY

Creating Outlines / Practice

Instructions: Practicing outlining an already-written paragraph can help you learn how to properly structure your own outline. Use the paragraph below to fill in the outline. Some of the information has already been filled in to help you get started.

1. One way to succeed in school is to use a planner or agenda. A planner helps students keep track of due dates and stay organized with their time. By using a planner, students visualize each activity in their day and can plan accordingly. If they notice that they have a test on Thursday and Friday, they know that they need to plan ahead to begin studying. In order to use a planner effectively, students must write any new assignments, tests, or quizzes into it daily. They also need to make sure it stays with them through the school day and get it out each afternoon or evening when they begin their homework.

I. ______________________________

A. How it helps

1. ______________________________

2. ______________________________

3. ______________________________

4. ______________________________

B. How to use it

1. ______________________________

2. ______________________________

3. ______________________________

ACTIVITY

Creating Outlines / Practice

Instructions: Practicing outlining an already-written paragraph can help you learn how to properly structure your own outline. Use the paragraph below to fill in the outline. Some of the information has already been filled in to help you get started.

1. Dogs make great pets because they provide comfort to their owners. They have an innate ability to provide emotional support by simply being there. Coming home to a dog's wagging tail immediately takes the edge off a stressful day. Many dogs can sense when people are feeling anxious or depressed, and they'll nuzzle up close to their owners. Their warm bodies and soft fur are incredibly calming. Dogs also reduce loneliness. They give the owner someone to come home to, take walks with, or simply sit with in silence. By having a dog around, a person will never be without a friend.

I. ______________________________

A. Provide emotional support

1. ______________________________

2. ______________________________

3. ______________________________

B. ______________________________

1. ______________________________

2. Someone to take walks with

3. ______________________________

ROMAN SENATE

As we learn from and imitate great authors, philosophers, and leaders we must take care to recognize the effort of those who have come before us by always citing our sources .

Fresco by Cesare Maccari

CHAPTER

Incorporating Research

ROADMAP

- Define plagiarism.
- Learn how to paraphrase and quote correctly.
- Distinguish between paraphrasing and summarizing.
- Learn how to cite properly and create an MLA Works Cited page.
- Practice identifying plagiarism.
- Practice creating in-text and bibliographic entries.

THALES OUTCOME

Nº 1

Unfailing Integrity *compels a person to follow a strong code of ethics with honesty in all situations.*

Integrity is at the heart of citing your sources. You must be honest in all you do, citing from only the most reputable sources and always giving credit to any outside source.

Citing Sources in MLA Format

TO BEGIN WITH, what is a citation? A **citation** is a reference of the source where you read, heard, or saw the information you are presenting in your paper.

We must give credit to the sources where we find our information for many reasons: to show our appreciation for that author's effort, to give credibility to our information, and to allow people to look further into our topic by reading from the sources we provide. If you fail to properly cite your information, you commit an act of academic dishonesty known as **plagiarism**.

Plagiarism is an act of academic dishonesty where you do not give proper credit to the source of your information. You must understand what plagiarism is so that you can avoid committing it.

There are many different ways that plagiarism occurs. You probably know you should not copy an essay from somewhere else and turn it in as if you wrote it yourself. However, plagiarism can be committed other ways as well.

Here are various examples of plagiarism:

1. Turning in someone else's work as your own.
2. Copying words or ideas from someone else without giving credit.
3. Failing to put a quotation in quotation marks, even if you provided the source information.
4. Giving incorrect information about the source of a quotation.
5. Changing words but copying the sentence structure of an excerpt from a source, even if you provided the source information.
6. Incorporating so many words or ideas from a source that it makes up the majority of your work, even if you provided the source information.

To avoid plagiarism, one thing we must always do is cite properly. When you cite a source, you give the details regarding where you found your information. Citations require specific, special formating.

Citing sources is necessary for many reasons: it recognizes the authors whose works you are using, it legitimizes your information, and it allows the readers of your essay to verify and find your sources for themselves.

Vocabulary

Citation
A mention of the source where you read, heard, or saw the information you are referencing.

Plagiarism
An act of academic dishonesty where you do not give proper credit to the source of your information, or you give credit but do not properly quote or paraphrase.

Works cited page
A page included at the end of your essay that lists all the sources you used in your research, formatted in a particular way.

In-text citations
Citations in the body of the essay that show the reader which source each fact or idea came from.

MLA Formatting

Now that we know what citations refer to, let's discuss the details of forming proper citations. In this book, we will focus on the MLA method for citations. There are many other methods for citing sources such as Chicago and APA, but those you will learn in future years. MLA formatting is a common format to learn first and is often used in literary writing.

Works Cited List

In all essays that include research, you must create a **works cited page** and use **in-text citations**. A works cited page is added after the last page of your essay and provides a list of all the resources you used for your information. It can include books, articles, videos, slideshows, and more. The idea of the works cited page is to give your readers enough information to verify the credibility of the source and read it for themselves, if they would like. You include information such as the author, title, and publisher.

There are many very specific rules that you must follow when creating a works cited page, so we will not go into all the details here. Use an MLA reference guide or resources provided by your teacher to help you. One excellent source, Purdue University's Online Writing Lab, contains up-to-date information on creating citations in both MLA and APA formatting. Here are a couple sample citations to give you an idea of what they look like, beginning with a book:

> Twain, Mark. *Adventures of Huckleberry Finn.* New York: Dover Publications Inc., 1885. Print.

And here is a sample citation of an article:

> Díez-del-Molino, David, et al. "Genomics of Adaptive Evolution in the Woolly Mammoth." *Current Biology*, vol. 33, no. 9, 8 May 2023, pp. 1753–1764, https://doi.org/10.1016/j.cub.2023.03.084. Accessed 1 Nov. 2024.

You can see how there are a lot of elements to include when creating a citation, but ultimately it allows your readers to easily see where you got your information and find it for themselves.

In-text citations

In-text citations appear within your essay itself directly after any information you include from a source. After the last word of your sentence, add parentheses and the source information, followed by the period that ends the sentence. The idea is to provide enough information that your reader can tell which source listed on your works cited page you are referencing. Specifically, you put the author's last name and the page number the information was found on. Some sources, such as webpages, do not have page numbers. In that case, you simply do not include a page number in the parentheses. If the source was an article that did not list an author, you instead put the name of the article. We will examine each of these possible types of in-text citations below.

Let's look at an article titled "The Importance of Teaching Poetry" by Nancy Martin Bailey. Below you will see the entry that would appear on the works cited page and the original passage:

> Bailey, Nancy Martin. "The Importance of Teaching Poetry." *Journal of Aesthetic Education*, vol. 23, no. 4, 1989, pp. 51-62.
>
> Sentence that appeared on page 62:
> *Poetry, no less than calculus, challenges our minds in ways that broaden our tolerance of complexity and enhance our comprehension of abstractions—reason enough to include a serious study of poetry in the curriculum.*

Let's imagine you wanted to incorporate this information into an essay about the study of poetry. This article has an author (Nancy Martin Bailey) and page numbers. We would include both the author's last name and the page where the information appeared, either in our sentence or in parentheses at the end of the sentence. Here are a few examples of how we would use an in-text citation when referencing ideas from this article:

In-text Citations with Author and Page Number
Poetry helps strengthen our ability to process and understand abstract information (Bailey 62).
According to Bailey, poetry helps strengthen our ability to process and understand abstract information (62).
Bailey states on page 62 that "poetry, no less than calculus, challenges our minds."

Vocabulary

Paraphrase
Information from a source that you wrote in your own words and sentence structure.

Quotation
A passage taken verbatim (word-for-word) from a source around which you place quotation marks.

Verbatim
The exact same words that were used in an original passage.

Ellipsis
The symbol of three periods in a row to show that a word or words have been left out of a direct quotation.

Brackets
The symbol [ ] used to show that a word was added to the original quotation to allow it to be grammatically correct.

In the examples, you see both paraphrases of the information (the first two examples) and a quotation (the third example). Whether you **paraphrase** or **quote** the information does not affect how you cite that information. In every sentence above, both the author's last name and the page number appear somewhere. You can incorporate that information into the sentence, in parentheses at the end of the sentence, or a little of each.

Now, sometimes an article will have an author, but no page number as in this next example. If that is the case, include the author's last name as before, but leave out the page number.

Simmons, Andrew. "Why Teaching Poetry Is so Important." *The Atlantic,* Atlantic Media Company, 8 Apr. 2014, www.theatlantic.com/education/archive/2014/04/why-teaching-poetry-is-so-important/360346/.

Sentence from article:
Poetry enables teachers to teach their students how to write, read, and understand any text. Poetry can give students a healthy outlet for surging emotions.

In-text Citations with Author and No Page Number

A benefit of studying poetry is that it allows students to process their feeling in a productive and controlled way (Simmons).

Simmons writes, "Poetry enables teachers to teach their students how to write, read, and understand any text."

Finally, you may want to cite an article that has neither an author nor a page number. First, make sure it's reliable following the rules we discussed earlier. If the article is reliable but does not have an author or page number, you include the title of the article instead. Here is an example of an article that did not name a specific author:

"Why Poetry Matters." *Scholastic Parents,* Scholastic, 7 Jun. 2023, www.scholastic.com/parents/books-and-reading/raise-a-reader-blog/why-poetry-matters.html.

Sentences from article:
Poetry helps children appreciate simple ideas through figurative language and gain a deeper understanding of stories outside of their own life experiences. By providing a window into the thoughts of others, poetry has the power to increase empathy and provide a new perspective of the human experience.

In-text Citations with No Author or Page Number

"Poetry has the power to increase empathy and provide a new perspective of the human experience" ("Why Poetry Matters").

In "Why Poetry Matters" the author states that poetry can improve students' empathy by encouraging them to see different points of view.

Students often mistakingly cite the website instead of the article title. You only need to include the website if you have more than one article with the exact same title. In this case you would still include the article title, but you would also include the website. That way, we can distinguish which source on your works cited page it is referring to. If you have further questions about this concept, consult a style manual or ask your teacher.

In all of these examples of in-text citations, we have included both paraphrases and direct quotations. Even if you cite your source, if you do not use quotation marks correctly or paraphrase correctly, you are still committing plagiarism. Let's discuss how to correctly incorporate your research into your essay through quotations and paraphrases in order to avoid plagiarism.

Quotations

A quotation is when you provide the exact words from a source. When you provide the wording **verbatim**, you must put quotation marks around those words. Even if you only use a few words from the source, if it is the exact same wording, you must use quotation marks. After the quotation, put your in-text, parenthetical citation, followed by a period. Below is a citation and two sentences taken directly from the article:

Díez-del-Molino, David, et al. "What Made Woolly Mammoths Ice Age Icons?" *Science Journal for Kids*, Oct. 2023, https://www.sciencejournalforkids.org/wp-content/uploads/2023/11/mammoth_article.pdf.

People have discovered preserved mammoth bodies in the frozen ground in Siberia. Their teeth and tusks remains are so well-preserved that they contain DNA scientists can study.

Let's see what it would look like to incorporate quotations from this source into our writing. Here are some examples:

Incorporating Quotes

According to Díez-del-Molino, "People have discovered preserved mammoth bodies in the frozen ground in Siberia."

Because the ground is frozen, the fossils of the woolly mammoths "are so well-preserved that they contain DNA scientists can study" (Díez-del-Molino).

"People have discovered preserved mammoth bodies...[that] are so well-preserved that they contain DNA scientists can study" (Díez-del-Molino).

Notice that our sentences contained words other than the exact words of the passage. If you include other words besides what is part of the direct quote, you do not put quotation marks around it. You only put quotation marks around those words that appear exactly the same as in the source.

The third example demonstrates the use of **ellipses** (...) and **brackets** ([ ]). If you want to incorporate two different parts of the article, but don't need the words in between, you can use an ellipsis to show that you have left information out. On the other hand, if you need to add a word or two to make the sentence more clear or grammatically correct when you are quoting just a portion of a sentence, you can use brackets. In doing so, make sure that you are not changing the meaning of any of the sentences or taking any information out of context.

Paraphrasing

Instead of quoting a passage directly, it is often better to **paraphrase**. Paraphrasing is when you include information from a source in your own words and sentence structure instead of as a direct quote. In this case, you do not use quotation marks because the source is not quoted verbatim; however, you must still give credit to the source through an in-text citation.

To create a proper paraphrase, you must put the information fully into your own words. This means that you must change both the wording and the sentence structure. You cannot simply take a quote and substitute synonyms for the words and call it a paraphrase. You must put the information entirely into your own writing, which includes how the sentence is structured. As we learned in Chapter 9, a lot of effort goes into creating a well-structured sentence. By keeping the original sentence structure of a passage and just changing the words, you are claiming the author's hard work as your own. This means that you also cannot just flip two halves of the sentence or combine or split sentences when paraphrasing. Instead, think about the *concepts* you want to convey and then put those ideas into your own words.

Let's look at two examples of ***incorrect*** paraphrasing:

Original Passage	Still Plagiarism
Original Passage: The Revolutionary War, also known as the American Revolution, arose from growing tensions between residents of Great Britain's 13 North American colonies and the colonial government, which represented the British crown.	*Still Plagiarism:* The American Revolution started from increasing friction between Great Britain's 13 North American colonies and the colonial government, which represented the English monarchy (History.com Editors).
Although there is an in-text citation and some words have been changed such as "started" instead of "arose," the overall structure of the sentences has stayed the same; therefore, this is still plagiarism.	
Original Passage: Woolly mammoths are extinct today, but they thrived during the Late Pleistocene era.	*Still Plagiarism:* Although woolly mammoths flourished in the Late Pleistocene era, they are extinct nowadays (Díez-del-Molino et al.).
Although there is an in-text citation and the halves of the sentence have been swapped, the structure within each section has not been changed, and many words are still the same; therefore, this is still plagiarism.	

Although the sentences in the previous chart have citations and some different words, they have not been fully written in this author's own words and structure; therefore, these still commit plagiarism.

Now, let's use these same passages to create a proper paraphrase:

Original Passage	Proper Paraphrasing
Original Passage: The Revolutionary War, also known as the American Revolution, arose from growing tensions between residents of Great Britain's 13 North American colonies and the colonial government, which represented the British crown.	*Proper Paraphrase:* The people of the thirteen colonies could not reconcile their differences with the British government, which ultimately led to the Revolutionary War (History.com Editors).
This paraphrase conveys the same information as the passage, but it has been written in an entirely new structure with different wording.	
Original Passage: Woolly mammoths are extinct today, but they thrived during the Late Pleistocene era.	*Proper Paraphrase:* The Late Pleistocene era, which ended approximately 11,700 years ago is known for the woolly mammoth, who flourished during that time (Díez-del-Molino et al.).
This paraphrase has also been written in an entirely new structure with different wording. Notice also, that the paraphrase included additional material from elsewhere in the article.	

To paraphrase correctly and avoid plagiarism, take shorthand notes of facts and ideas, not full sentences. If you have only facts listed, it is much easier to incorporate those facts into your essay in your own words. In addition, don't try to take just one sentence and paraphrase it. Instead, think of the article as a whole, and incorporate multiple pieces of information into one sentence. This method will make it much easier to write the information with your own sentence structure.

Now, notice that we have discussed direct quotations, which keeps the wording exactly the same, and paraphrasing, which involves fully changing the wording and structure of the sentences. You can either quote information from a source verbatim or you can fully alter the words and structure. That means that you can never change just a few words and still avoid plagiarizing. If you change a few words, you can no longer use quotation marks, but you have also not put the information into your own unique sentence. You must either fully and properly paraphrase, or you must keep the wording exactly the same and use quotation marks.

You do have the option of both quoting and paraphrasing in the same sentence. You may keep a few of the words exactly the same and then change the wording in the rest of the sentence. In this case, you would put your quotation marks around the portion that is quoted verbatim, and then put your citation at the end of the whole sentence.

Punctuation Rules

Before we finish our discussion of citations, let's review punctuation rules that go with them. When you write quotations and in-text citations, there are 3 things to remember:

1. If there is a parenthetical citation at the end of the sentence, there should only be a period after the final parentheses.
2. If there is no parenthetical citation, the period goes after the last word of the sentence, before any quotation marks.
3. Article titles should be in quotation marks.

Let's return to some of our earlier examples to examine how they were punctuated:

Punctuating Quotations and Paraphrases

According to Díez-del-Molino, "People have discovered preserved mammoth bodies in the frozen ground in Siberia."

Notice how the period is after the last word, before *the quotation mark.*

Because the ground is frozen, the fossils of the woolly mammoths "are so well-preserved that they contain DNA scientists can study" (Díez-del-Molino).

Notice how the quotation mark is after the last word of the quote, and there is not a period at the end of the quote. Because there is a parenthetical citation, the period is after the last parenthesis.

Poetry can improve students' empathy by encouraging them to see different points-of-view ("Why Poetry Matters").

Notice how there is not a period at the end of the paraphrase. Because there is a parenthetical citation, the period is after the last parenthesis. Notice also that the title of the article has quotation marks around it.

So remember, give credit to your sources and write with your own words, and you will create a unique essay free of plagiarism but full of strong evidence.

Reading Comprehension Questions

1. What is plagiarism? How do you avoid plagiarizing in a research essay?

2. What is a works cited page?

3. What are in-text citations? How do you write them?

4. How do you properly paraphrase?

ACTIVITY

Creating Works Cited Entries / Practice

Instructions: For each link provided, find the information listed. Then, with the help of a citation guide or handouts from your teacher, create an MLA works cited entry for that source.

1. https://www.britannica.com/biography/Galileo-Galilei

Author: ______________________________

Title of article: ______________________________

Name of container/organization: ______________________________

Name of publisher: ______________________________

Last updated: ______________________________

Works Cited entry: ______________________________

____

2. https://www.history.com/topics/us-presidents/thomas-jefferson

Author: ______________________________

Title of article: ______________________________

Name of container/organization: ______________________________

Name of publisher: ______________________________

Last updated: ______________________________

Works Cited entry: ______________________________

____

ACTIVITY

Creating Works Cited Entries / Practice

Instructions: For each link provided, find the information listed. Then, with the help of a citation guide or handouts from your teacher, create an MLA works cited entry for that source.

3. https://www.sciencenews.org/article/zigzag-walls-help-buildings-beat-heat

Author: ______________________________

Title of article: ______________________________

Name of container/organization: ______________________________

Name of publisher: ______________________________

Last updated: ______________________________

Works Cited entry: ______________________________

____

4. https://www.usnews.com/education/k12/articles/the-benefits-of-arts-education-for-k-12-students

Author: ______________________________

Title of article: ______________________________

Name of container/organization: ______________________________

Name of publisher: ______________________________

Last updated: ______________________________

Works Cited entry: ______________________________

____

ACTIVITY

Adding In-text Citations / Practice

Instructions: For each source below, you have been given five sentences that contain information from that source. Write the sentence, adding MLA formatted in-text citation information as needed and proper punctuation. You do not need to change the wording of any of the sentences.

Source: LaVaque, Kendall. "The Importance of Reading Classic Literature: Why These Books Stand the Test of Time." *Medium*, 3 May 2023.

1. Reading classic literature "allows us to gain a deeper understanding of the human experience."

____

____

2. Kendall states, "These books challenge our intellect and force us to think deeply about complex issues."

____

____

3. Classic literature exposes students to various cultures.

____

____

4. Reading the classics creates more well-rounded students.

____

____

5. Classic literature "deal[s] with issues such as love, loss, betrayal, and redemption."

____

____

ACTIVITY

Adding In-text Citations / Practice

Instructions: For each source below, you have been given five sentences that contain information from that source. Write the sentence, adding MLA formatted in-text citation information as needed and proper punctuation. You do not need to change the wording of any of the sentences.

Source: Greenspan, Jesse. "How the Declaration of Independence Was Printed and Protected." *History.com*, 28 Jun. 2022.

1. On July 4, 1776, John Dunlap printed approximately 200 smaller sized copies of the Declaration of Independence.

____

____

2. The protection that Declaration of Independence receives now is a "newfound development."

____

____

3. "Though birthed in Philadelphia," it traveled with the Continental Congress around multiple states.

____

____

4. The Declaration continued to be moved around because of various wars and conflicts.

____

____

5. According to Greenspan, it has been housed in the National Archives since 1952.

____

____

JEAN MIÉLOT

This picture shows Jean Miélot, a European author and scribe at work in a writing room.

Art by Jean Le Tavernier

CHAPTER

Writing the Research Essay

ROADMAP

- Discover ways to organize your research essay.
- Learn the ICE method for incorporating research.
- Discuss vocabulary and sentence structure in research writing.
- Write a research paper.

THALES OUTCOME

Nº 2

A **Virtuous Leader** *with Well-Developed Judgment combines thinking skills and traits such as humility, generosity, and courage*

Learning to write a well-developed research paper will help you become a better, more capable leader. The research process teaches you how to find and evaluate information and present it to your audience in a logical manner.

Writing the Research Essay

YOU ARE NOW READY to begin writing your research essay. The actual process of writing a research essay is not much different from any other essay. Your introduction should still begin with a hook, followed by any necessary background information, and end with your thesis statement. Your conclusion should contain a summary and end with a clincher. And when you revise, you should edit for organization and flow, word choice, and sentence fluency.

Primarily, your research will affect your body paragraphs. Recall that each of your body paragraphs should begin with a claim, followed by evidence, analysis, and a wrap-up. The "evidence" element is the primary spot where you will incorporate your research.

First, your body paragraphs should not start or end with research information or quotations. The beginning and end of each body paragraph should be claims and wrap-ups. Remember, even though you are incorporating information from your research into your essay, you are still presenting your own reasons and ideas. You should begin your body paragraph with your own claim, not a researched fact, quotation, or someone else's claim. After you present your claim, then incorporate your evidence. At this point, include those facts from your research which back up your claim. After that, you explain or analyze that information

The **ICE** method will help you properly incorporate your research into your essay. ICE is an acronym for Introduce, Cite, and Explain. Whenever you present research information in the form of a quotation or a paraphrase, you must first introduce that information. You can use phrases like "according to" or provide context for the information. Then, present the quotation or paraphrase and cite that information as we discussed in the previous chapter. Finally, you must not forget to explain or analyze that information. Just like we have practiced in your non-research essays, you must always analyze the evidence you present, explaining how it helps prove your claim.

Let's examine a small body paragraph written in this format:

One primary benefit of reading classical literature is that these books have abiding themes. As LaVaque points out, common themes include "love, loss, betrayal, and redemption." By reading books with these themes, students gain a deeper understanding of their own lives.

The actual process of writing the sentences of your research paper is not much different from any other expository essay or persuasive essay. The primary difference is that the evidence you present comes from research you have conducted.

Vocabulary

ICE
A method of incorporating quotations or paraphrase where you introduced, cite, and explain the information.

The first sentence in the example on the previous page presents the claim of the paragraph: we should read the classics because of their enduring themes. The second sentence introduces the quotation by saying ***As LaVaque points out***. This also serves as the citation by presenting the author of the article. (This information came from an online article that did not have page numbers, so no additional parenthetical citation is necessary.) This quotation serves as one piece of evidence for the paragraph—the themes around which classic literature revolves. Then, the third sentence analyzes this idea by saying how reading books with these themes benefit students.

Often, you will repeat this ICE method more than once in a paragraph because you are including more than one piece of evidence to support your claim. Additionally, you can have more than one source to support your information. Perhaps you found another source that included additional themes that classical literature teaches. You can include information from both sources before analyzing them together.

A research essay can be written for a variety of purposes. In an expository research essay, your goal would be to research a topic and then inform the reader about that topic. You might write an expository essay on the life of Julius Caesar, the inventions Benjamin Franklin, or the history of the Brooklyn Bridge.

You can also write a research essay whose purpose is to persuade. In fact, most persuasive essays are research essays because you strengthen your argument by citing well-researched facts. Without research, your argument is based solely on your own opinions, experiences, or general reasoning.

As you advance to high school and move in higher education, most essays you write will include research. As we have discussed, make sure you only use reputable, verified information, incorporate the research into your own words, and cite all your sources properly.

ESSAY

Research Essay / Assignment

Instructions: You are writing a five-paragraph expository research essay on one of the topics below. You will support your thesis with three strong reasons.

Topic Choices
1. *Choose a virtuous leader that you have studied in history this year. Give an overview of his or her life, with a focus on why he or she deserves to be called virtuous leader.*
2. *Choose a famous person who lived during a time and place you have studied in school this year. Choose three topics that you believe were the most significant in that person's life.*
3. *Choose a particular place that relates to your study of history this year. Discuss the place's history and what it is known for.*
4. *Choose a particular discovery or invention that was created in a time and place which you have studied in school this year. Write an essay on the development and significance of that invention.*
5. *Choose an author whose work you have read for school this year. Write an essay on his or her life with a focus on how they came to be a writer or write that particular book.*

Essay Guidelines

- *Introduction and conclusion, each of which contains at least three sentences.*
- *Three body paragraphs of at least five sentences that each contain one reason/idea in support of your thesis.*
- *Essay should be in MLA format, including in-text citations and a works cited page.*
- *Essay should be free of grammatical and spelling errors.*
- *You should use research from at least three reliable sources in the body of your essay.*
- *Research should be incorporated using the ICE method and quoting or paraphrasing correctly.*
- *Essay should be well-organized, written solely in third-person, and free of contractions.*
- *Writing should be organized, use a specific and detailed vocabulary with a variety of sentence structures that improve the essay's overall rhythm.*

To review guidelines of what should be included in each paragraph, see appropriate chapters in this textbook and view the grading rubric on the next page.

ESSAY

Grading Rubric / Research Essay after Chapter 9

Below are the elements you will be graded on. Details regarding each of these elements are outlined in earlier chapters.

Essay Component	*Criteria*	*Notes*
MLA Formatting	General Formatting ____/5	
Introduction	Hook ____/5 Background/connection____/5 Thesis _____/5	
Organization	Transitions ____/5 Paragraphs ____/5 Claims ____/5	
Evidence	Quotations introduced/explained _____/5 Quality evidence/analysis _____/10	
Citations	MLA In-text citations _____/10 MLA works cited page _____/10	
Conclusion	Summary ____/5 Clincher ____/5	
Overall Elements	Word Choice ____/10 Sentence Fluency ____/10	

TOTAL: ______/100

Fall foggy forest landscape

By Veneratio

APPENDIX

Appendix

CONTENTS

ACTIVITY

Research Notes Sheet

Use this space to record your research notes on your topic.

Link to resource used:	
Author:	
Title:	

Notes:

Link to resource used:	
Author:	
Title:	

Notes:

ACTIVITY

Brainstorming Web

Use this space to create a brainstorming web for your topic.

ACTIVITY

Writing the Thesis Statement

Instructions: Use the flowchart below to draft and revise a thesis statement. This is the flow chart to use when first and second person point-of-view is prohibited.

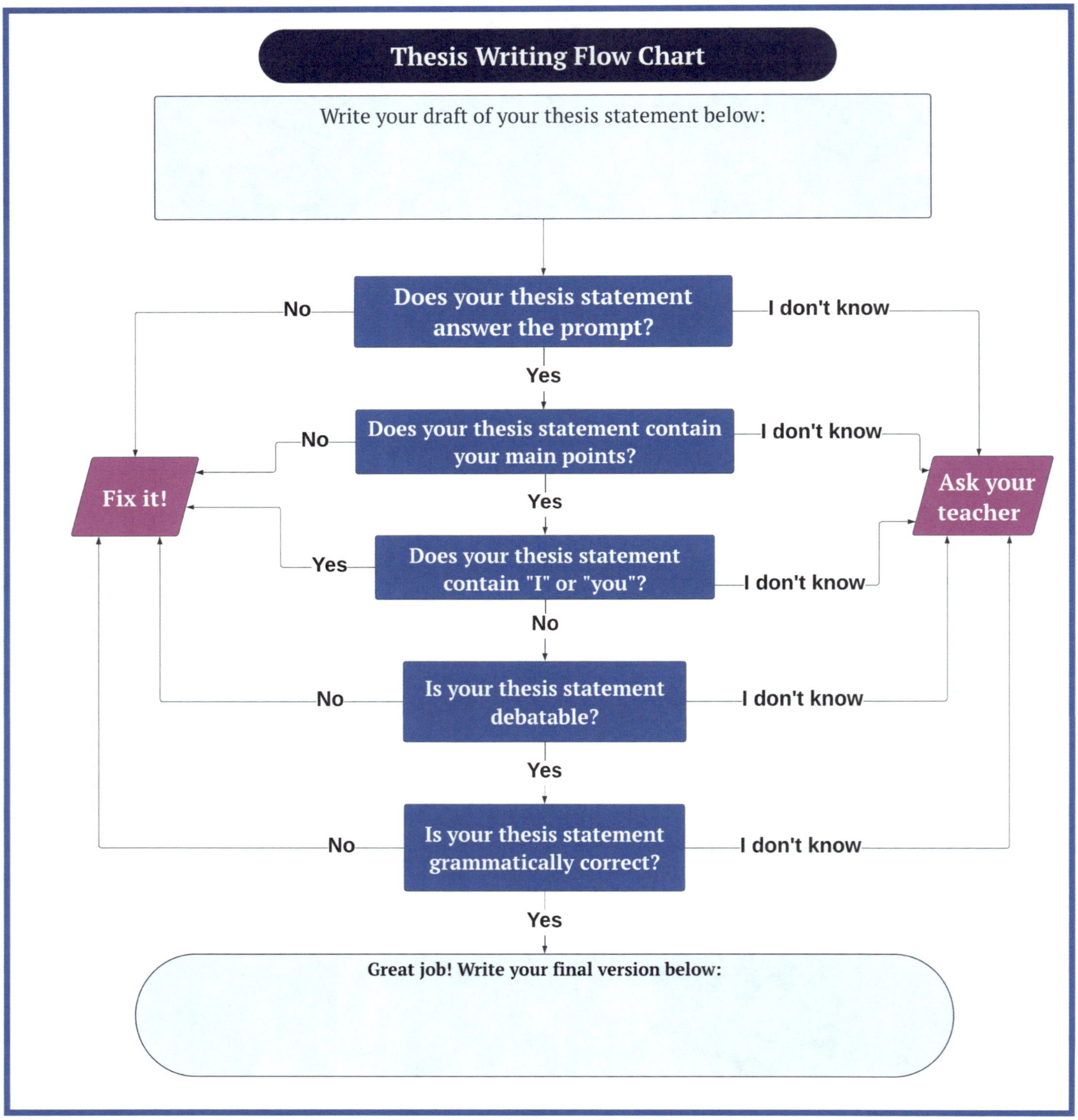

Thesis Writing Flow Chart

Write your draft of your thesis statement below:

Does your thesis statement answer the prompt?
- No → Fix it!
- I don't know → Ask your teacher
- Yes ↓

Does your thesis statement contain your main points?
- No → Fix it!
- I don't know → Ask your teacher
- Yes ↓

Does your thesis statement contain "I" or "you"?
- Yes → Fix it!
- I don't know → Ask your teacher
- No ↓

Is your thesis statement debatable?
- No → Fix it!
- I don't know → Ask your teacher
- Yes ↓

Is your thesis statement grammatically correct?
- No → Fix it!
- I don't know → Ask your teacher
- Yes ↓

Great job! Write your final version below:

ACTIVITY

Writing the Thesis Statement / Flowchart

Instructions: Use the flowchart below to draft and revise a thesis statement. This is the flow chart to use when first and second person point-of-view is permitted.

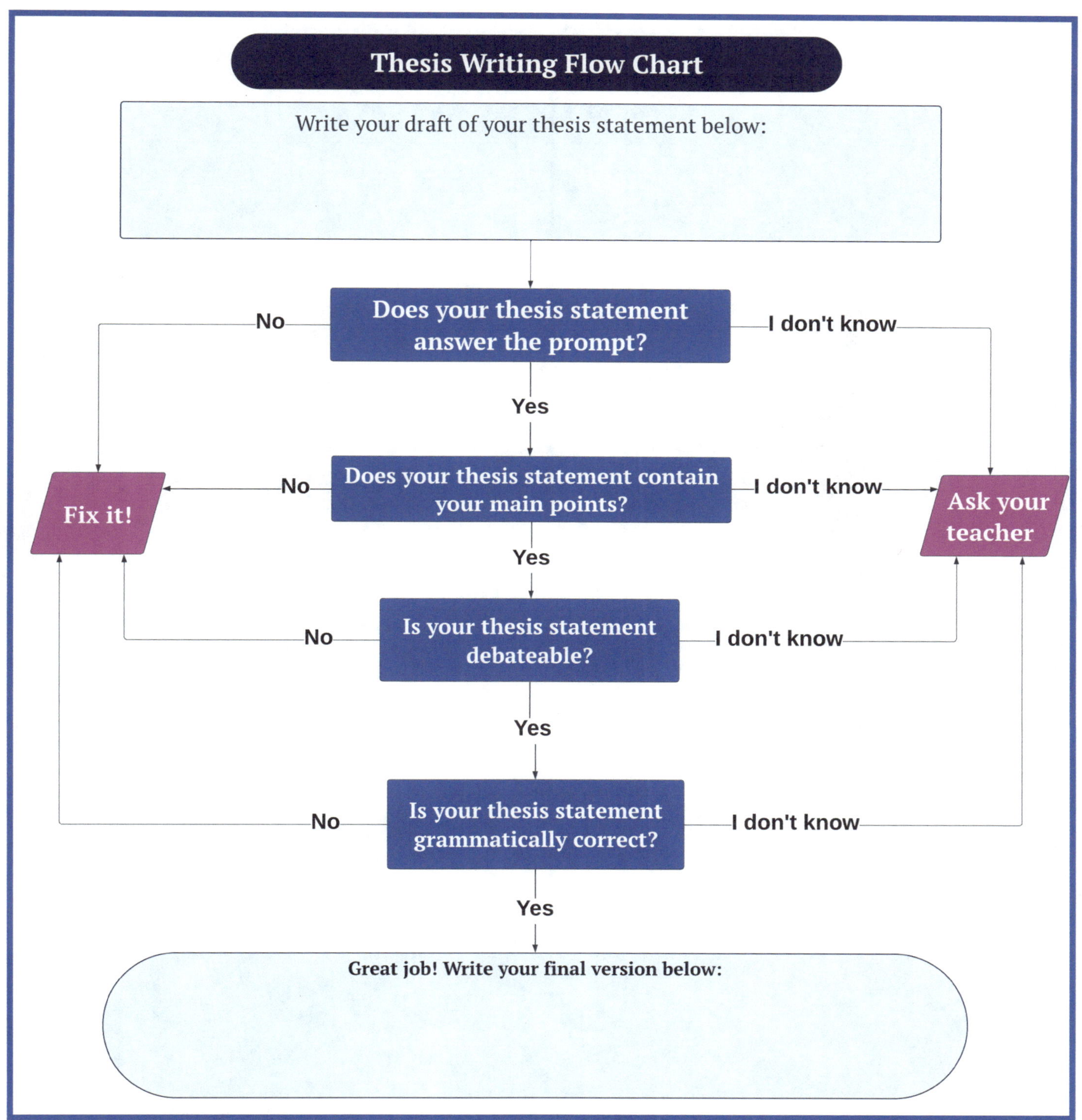

ACTIVITY

Essay Map

Use the following essay map to outline your main points after you have determined your thesis.

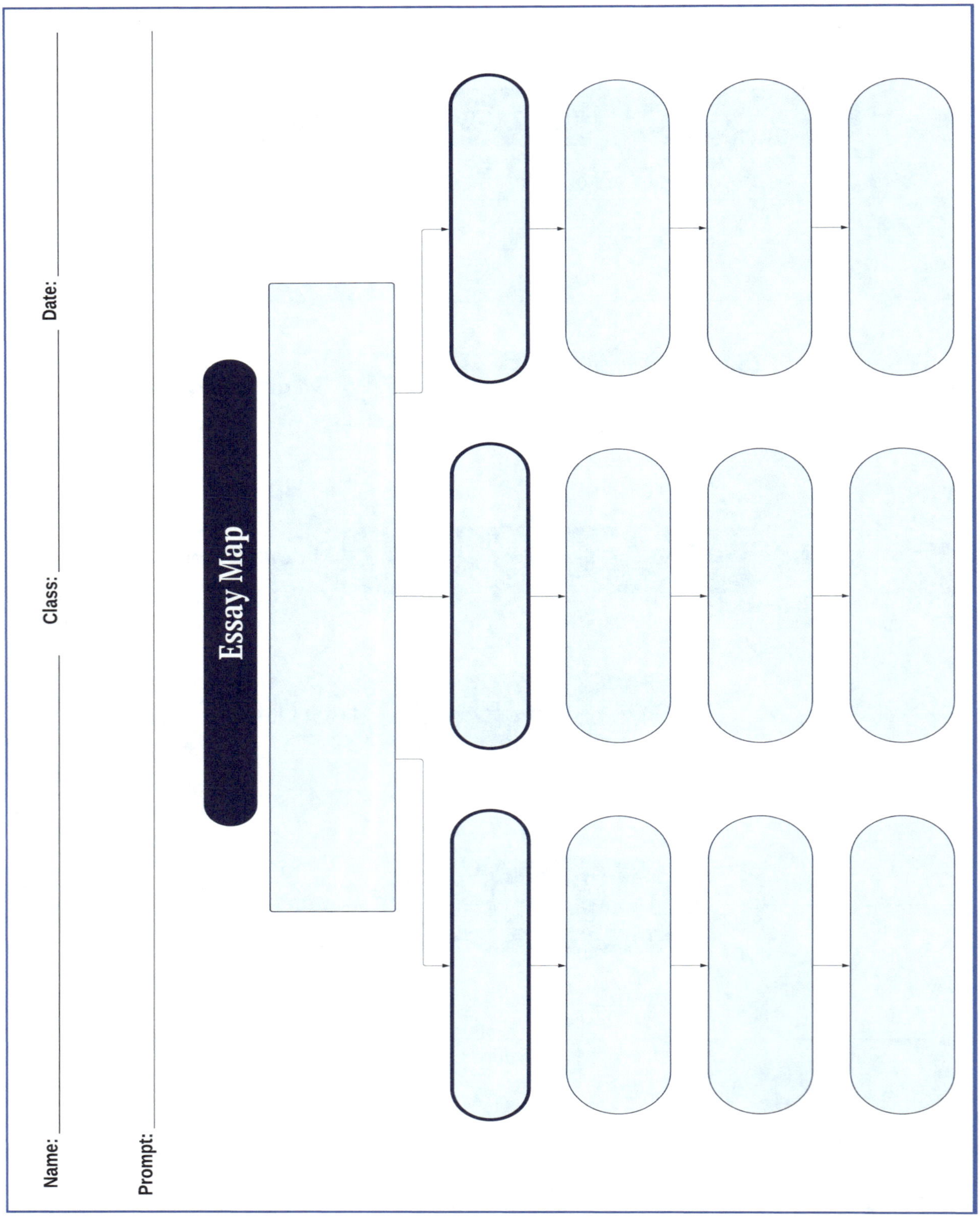

Name: ____________ Class: ____________ Date: ____________

Prompt: ____________

Essay Map

5-Paragraph Essay / Summary

The chart below summarizes each of the paragraphs in a 5-paragraph expository essay. See Chapter 4 (introductions), 5 (body paragraphs), and 6 (conclusions) for additional details on how to write these paragraphs.

Paragraph 1: The Introduction	
Sentence	***Explanation***
1	**Hook:** A sentence that catches your reader's attention. Questions, interesting facts, anecdotes, quotations, and metaphors can all make good hooks.
2	**Connecting Sentence:** A sentence to lead from your hook to your thesis
3	**Thesis Statement:** 1-2 sentences that presents your claim about the topic and your three main points. You should have already created this, so now you just have to type it down again.

Paragraph 2: Body Paragraph 1	
Sentence	***Explanation***
1	**Claim:** A sentence which states your topic and your first main point (i.e. "I want to be a teacher because I want to inspire my students.")
Varies	**Evidence:** A sentence to prove your claim. There can be multiple evidence sentences.
Varies	**Analysis:** A sentence to explain your evidence, if needed.
Last sentence	**Wrap-up:** A sentence to restate or summarize the main point of this paragraph

Paragraph 3: Body Paragraph 2
REPEAT ABOVE STEPS FOR 2ND MAIN POINT

Paragraph 4: Body Paragraph 3
REPEAT ABOVE STEPS FOR 3RD MAIN POINT

Paragraph 5: The Conclusion (From chapter 6)	
Sentence	Explanation
1-2	**Summary:** Two sentences that summarize the main points of your essay. It should be slightly more detailed than your thesis.
3	**Clincher:** The final sentence of your essay that gives a meaningful send-off to your reader. Some types of clinchers include creating bookends by complementing your hook, answering the question "So what?" about your argument, considering the broader implications of your argument, or giving your reader a "Call to Action."

Self-Evaluation / 5-paragraph Essay Draft (for use after chapter 5)

Use this evaluation rubric to score the content of your essay draft in each of the following categories. In each blank, give yourself a score out of three points. Be thoughtful and honest in your reflection - that is how you are going to improve. In the reflection column, explain why you gave yourself that score.

Essay Component	*Criteria*	*Reflection*
Introduction 3 points each _____ / 9 points	_____ Hook _____ Connecting hook to thesis _____ Thesis statement	
1st Body Paragraph 3 points each _____ / 12 points	____ Claim ____ Analysis ____ Evidence ____ Wrap-up	
2nd Body Paragraph 3 points each _____ / 12 points	____ Claim ____ Analysis ____ Evidence ____ Wrap-up	
3rd Body Paragraph 3 points each _____ / 12 points	____ Claim ____ Analysis ____ Evidence ____ Wrap-up	
Conclusion 3 points each _____ / 6 points	_____ Summary _____ Clincher	

TOTAL: ______/51

Peer Evaluation / 5-paragraph Essay Draft (for use after chapter 5)

Use this evaluation rubric to score the content of your partner's draft in each of the categories. In each blank, give them a score out of three points. Be thoughtful and honest in your reflection - that is how you are going to help them improve. In the Explanation column, explain why you gave them that score

Essay Component	*Criteria*	*Explanation*
Introduction 3 points each _____ / 9 points	_____ Hook _____ Connecting hook to thesis _____ Thesis statement	
1st **Body Paragraph** 3 points each _____ / 12 points	____ Claim ____ Analysis ____ Evidence ____ Wrap-up	
2nd **Body Paragraph** 3 points each _____ / 12 points	____ Claim ____ Analysis ____ Evidence ____ Wrap-up	
3rd **Body Paragraph** 3 points each _____ / 12 points	____ Claim ____ Analysis ____ Evidence ____ Wrap-up	
Conclusion 3 points each _____ / 6 points	_____ Summary _____ Clincher	

TOTAL: ______/51

APPENDIX

Word Choice / Replacements for Vague Verbs

The first row of this chart lists 5 of the most commonly overused, vague verbs. Below each one, you will see alternatives to try. These words all have slightly different meanings. Be sure you understand the definition and connotation before using it in your writing.

Like/Love	Go/Went	See/Look	Get/Got	Say/Said
Enjoy	Proceed	Detect	Grab	Announce
Adore	Travel	Examine	Obtain	Answer
Cherish	Journey	Identify	Receive	Assert
Fancy	Adventure	Notice	Secure	Claim
Appreciate	Progress	Observe	Snag	Respond
Admire	Retire	Recognize	Capture	Suggest
Prefer	Flee	Regard	Apprehend	Reveal
Desire	Saunter	Peer	Seize	Mention
Elect	Stroll	Scan	Collect	Declare
Wish	Dash	Scrutinize	Earn	Estimate
Savor	Slitter	Gawk	Pocket	Voice
Treasure	Crawl	Glare	Accept	Allege
Relish	Hike	Inspect	Acquire	Divulge
Respect	Parade	Survey	Inherit	Relate
Prize	Traipse	Spy	Procure	Remark
Value	Roam	Note	Gain	Report
Honor	Trudge	Glimpse	Find	Reply
	Race	Study	Discover	
	Traverse	View	Locate	
	Rush		Unearth	
	Escape		Attain	
	Amble			
	Sprint			
	Depart			
	Hasten			

Word Choice / Persuasive Words

Strong verbs improve the persuasiveness of your writing. The chart below lists 85 persuasive verbs. You can use these as a starting point as you learn to improve your vocabulary. Feel free to add to this list when your come across other strong vocabulary words.

85 Persuasive Verbs				
Abolish	Connect	Illuminate	Inspire	Replace
Accelerate	Convert	Evaluate	Kindle	Resist
Achieve	Create	Evolve	Lead	Respond
Adopt	Define	Explore	Manage	Retain
Advance	Deliver	Extinguish	Master	Revolve
Advocate	Deploy	Finalize	Maximize	Simplify
Anticipate	Design	Focus	Motivate	Solve
Apply	Develop	Forge	Navigate	Succeed
Assess	Devour	Gain	Nurture	Supplement
Avoid	Diagnose	Gather	Overcome	Surge
Boost	Discover	Generate	Penetrate	Take
Bridge	Drive	Grapple	Persuade	Train
Build	Educate	Grasp	Prepare	Transfer
Capture	Eliminate	Identify	Prevent	Transform
Clarify	Ensure	Implement	Profit	Traverse
Comprehend	Establish	Improve	Propel	Unleash
Confront	Ignite	Increase	Reconsider	Yield

ESSAY

Self-Evaluation / Essay Revisions (for use after Chapter 9)

Use this evaluation form to score the content of your essay in each of the following categories. In each blank, give yourself a score out of three points. Be thoughtful and honest in your reflection - that is how you are going to improve. In the reflection column, explain why you gave yourself that score.

Essay Component	*Criteria*	*Reflection*
Organization 3 points each _____ / 9 points	_____ Only one point per paragraph _____ Use of transitions _____ Flow of thoughts	
Word Choice 3 points each _____ / 9 points	_____ Descriptive words _____ Active verbs _____ Specificity of words/connotation	
Sentence Structure 3 points each _____ / 9 points	_____ Sentence length _____ Sentence starters _____ Complexity of sentences	
Formatting 3 points each _____ / 9 points	_____ Header _____ Font (size/format/color) _____ Title	
Conventions 3 **points each** _____ / 9 points	_____ Grammar _____ Spelling _____ Point of view follows directions	

TOTAL: _______/45

Peer Evaluation / Essay Revisions (for use after Chapter 9)

Use this evaluation form to score your partner's essay in each of the categories. In each blank, give them a score out of three points. Be thoughtful and honest in your reflection - that is how you are going to help them improve. In the Explanation column, explain why you gave them that score.

Essay Component	*Criteria*	*Reflection*
Organization 3 points each _____ / 9 points	_____ Only one point per paragraph _____ Use of transitions _____ Flow of thoughts	
Word Choice 3 points each _____ / 9 points	_____ Descriptive words _____ Active verbs _____ Specificity of words/connotation	
Sentence Struc-ture 3 points each _____ / 9 points	_____ Sentence length _____ Sentence starters _____ Complexity of sentences	
Formatting 3 points each _____ / 9 points	_____ Header _____ Font (size/format/color) _____ Title	
Conventions 3 points each _____ / 9 points	_____ Grammar _____ Spelling _____ Point of view follows directions	

TOTAL: ______/45

TEMPLATE

Key Word Outline

Instructions: An outline provides a helpful way to organize your thoughts and get them on paper. The sample below shows you a way in which you can break down your points into a key word outline.

In this style of outline, you only write key words and phrases, not entire sentences. The page count on this style of outline should be quite long because you are starting so many new lines, but each line should only have a handful of words on it.

The subpoints under each main point will vary drastically between different outlines/essays. You may not need to split your main point into supporting ideas, so your capital letters become the evidence and the Arabic numerals become the explanation, if needed at all. Although learning the formatting can be tricky, structuring your outline in this way allows you to more easily see your points and evidence and how they work together. This, in turn, allows you to more easily analyze your ideas and see where they need to be restructured or where something may be lacking your argument.

I. Introductory Paragraph

- **A.** Hook - write the type of hook you will use and some key words of it here
- **B.** Background information or how you will transition from hook to thesis - key words only
- **C.** Thesis claim or topic - just a few words listed
    - **1.** First reason/topic in support of claim
    - **2.** Second reason/topic in support of claim
    - **3.** Third reason/topic in support of claim

II. First Main Point *(State key words of point)*

- **A. Supporting Idea:** *A sub-category of the main point of this paragraph*
    - **1.** Example/Evidence/Fact
        - **a.** Additional information/explanation if needed
        - **b.** Additional information/explanation
        - **c.** *Repeat as needed for additional explanation*
    - **2.** Example/Evidence/Fact
        - **a.** Additional information/explanation
        - **b.** Additional information/explanation
        - **c.** *Repeat as needed for additional explanation*
    - **3.** *Repeat arabic numerals for each fact/piece of evidence for this point*
- **B.** *Repeat as needed for additional supporting idea*

III. Second Main Point *(See directions above)*

II. Third Main Point *(See directions above)*

V. Conclusion

- **A.** Thesis Claim
    - **1.** Key words to summarize first point
    - **2.** Key words to summarize secondpoint
    - **3.** Key words to summarize third point
- **B.** Clincher/closing sentence - key words to explain what you want your reader to take away/remember

"The Road Not Taken" / By Robert Frost

Two roads diverged in a yellow wood,
And sorry I could not travel both
And be one traveller, long I stood
And looked down one as far as I could
To where it bent in the undergrowth;

Then took the other, as just as fair,
And having perhaps the better claim,
Because it was grassy and wanted wear;
Though as for that the passing there
Had worn them really about the same,

And both that morning equally lay
In leaves no step had trodden black.
Oh, I kept the first for another day!
Yet knowing how way leads on to way,
I doubted if I should ever come back.

I shall be telling this with a sigh
Somewhere ages and ages hence:
Two roads diverged in a wood, and I—
I took the one less travelled by,
And that has made all the difference.

"Going for Water" / By Robert Frost

The well was dry beside the door,
And so we went with pail and can
Across the fields behind the house
To seek the brook if still it ran;

Not loth to have excuse to go,
Because the autumn eve was fair
(Though chill), because the fields were ours,
And by the brook our woods were there.

We ran as if to meet the moon
That slowly dawned behind the trees,
The barren boughs without the leaves,
Without the birds, without the breeze.

But once within the wood, we paused
Like gnomes that hid us from the moon,
Ready to run to hiding new
With laughter when she found us soon.

Each laid on other a staying hand
To listen ere we dared to look,
And in the hush we joined to make
We heard, we knew we heard the brook.

A note as from a single place,
A slender tinkling fall that made
Now drops that floated on the pool
Like pearls, and now a silver blade.

"Sonnet 18" / By William Shakespeare

Shall I compare thee to a summer's day?
Thou art more lovely and more temperate:
Rough winds do shake the darling buds of May,
And summer's lease hath all too short a date;
Sometime too hot the eye of heaven shines,
And often is his gold complexion dimm'd;
And every fair from fair sometime declines,
By chance or nature's changing course untrimm'd;
But thy eternal summer shall not fade,
Nor lose possession of that fair thou ow'st;
Nor shall death brag thou wander'st in his shade,
When in eternal lines to time thou grow'st:
So long as men can breathe or eyes can see,
So long lives this, and this gives life to thee.

"How Do I Love Thee?" / Elizabeth Barrett Browning

How do I love thee? Let me count the ways.
I love thee to the depth and breadth and height
My soul can reach, when feeling out of sight
For the ends of being and ideal grace.
I love thee to the level of every day's
Most quiet need, by sun and candle-light.
I love thee freely, as men strive for right;
I love thee purely, as they turn from praise.
I love thee with the passion put to use
In my old griefs, and with my childhood's faith.
I love thee with a love I seemed to lose
With my lost saints. I love thee with the breath,
Smiles, tears, of all my life; and, if God choose,
I shall but love thee better after death.

"Dreams" / By Langston Hughes

Hold fast to dreams
For if dreams die
Life is a broken-winged bird
That cannot fly.

Hold fast to dreams
For when dreams go
Life is a barren field
Frozen with snow.

"O Captain! My Captain!" / By Walt Whitman

O Captain! my Captain! our fearful trip is done,
The ship has weather'd every rack, the prize we sought is won,
The port is near, the bells I hear, the people all exulting,
While follow eyes the steady keel, the vessel grim and daring;
But O heart! heart! heart!
O the bleeding drops of red,
Where on the deck my Captain lies,
Fallen cold and dead.

O Captain! my Captain! rise up and hear the bells;
Rise up—for you the flag is flung—for you the bugle trills,
For you bouquets and ribbon'd wreaths—for you the shores a-crowding,
For you they call, the swaying mass, their eager faces turning;
Here Captain! dear father!
This arm beneath your head!
It is some dream that on the deck,
You've fallen cold and dead.

My Captain does not answer, his lips are pale and still,
My father does not feel my arm, he has no pulse nor will,
The ship is anchor'd safe and sound, its voyage closed and done,
From fearful trip the victor ship comes in with object won;

Exult O shores, and ring O bells!
But I with mournful tread,
Walk the deck my Captain lies,
Fallen cold and dead.

"Because I Could Not Stop for Death" / Emily Dickenson

Because I could not stop for Death—
He kindly stopped for me—
The Carriage held but just Ourselves—
And Immortality.

We slowly drove—He knew no haste
And I had put away
My labor and my leisure too,
For His Civility—

We passed the School, where Children strove
At Recess—in the Ring—
We passed the Fields of Gazing Grain—
We passed the Setting Sun—

Or rather—He passed Us—
The Dews drew quivering and Chill—
For only Gossamer, my Gown—
My Tippet—only Tulle—

We paused before a House that seemed
A Swelling of the Ground—
The Roof was scarcely visible—
The Cornice—in the Ground—

Since then—'tis Centuries—and yet
Feels shorter than the Day
I first surmised the Horses' Heads
Were toward Eternity—

"She Walks in Beauty" by Lord Byron
She walks in beauty, like the night
Of cloudless climes and starry skies;
And all that's best of dark and bright
Meet in her aspect and her eyes;
Thus mellowed to that tender light
Which heaven to gaudy day denies.

One shade the more, one ray the less,
Had half impaired the nameless grace
Which waves in every raven tress,
Or softly lightens o'er her face;
Where thoughts serenely sweet express,
How pure, how dear their dwelling-place.

And on that cheek, and o'er that brow,
So soft, so calm, yet eloquent,
The smiles that win, the tints that glow,
But tell of days in goodness spent,
A mind at peace with all below,
A heart whose love is innocent!

"I Wandered Lonely as a Cloud" / By William Wordsworth

I wandered lonely as a cloud
That floats on high o'er vales and hills,
When all at once I saw a crowd,
A host, of golden daffodils;
Beside the lake, beneath the trees,
Fluttering and dancing in the breeze.

Continuous as the stars that shine
And twinkle on the milky way,
They stretched in never-ending line
Along the margin of a bay:
Ten thousand saw I at a glance,
Tossing their heads in sprightly dance.

The waves beside them danced; but they
Out-did the sparkling waves in glee:
A poet could not but be gay,
In such a jocund company:
I gazed—and gazed—but little thought
What wealth the show to me had brought:

For oft, when on my couch I lie
In vacant or in pensive mood,
They flash upon that inward eye
Which is the bliss of solitude;
And then my heart with pleasure fills,
And dances with the daffodils.

Selection from The Wasteland / By T. S. Eliot

April is the cruellest month, breeding
Lilacs out of the dead land, mixing
Memory and desire, stirring
Dull roots with spring rain.
Winter kept us warm, covering
Earth in forgetful snow, feeding
A little life with dried tubers.
Summer surprised us, coming over the Starnbergersee
With a shower of rain; we stopped in the colonnade,
And went on in sunlight, into the Hofgarten,
And drank coffee, and talked for an hour.
Bin gar keine Russin, stamm' aus Litauen, echt deutsch.
And when we were children, staying at the archduke's,
My cousin's, he took me out on a sled,
And I was frightened. He said, Marie,
Marie, hold on tight. And down we went.
In the mountains, there you feel free.
I read, much of the night, and go south in the winter.
And dances with the daffodils.

"Jabberwocky" / **Lewis Carroll**

'Twas brillig, and the slithy toves
Did gyre and gimble in the wabe:
All mimsy were the borogoves,
And the mome raths outgrabe.

"Beware the Jabberwock, my son!
The jaws that bite, the claws that catch!
Beware the Jubjub bird, and shun
The frumious Bandersnatch!"
He took his vorpal sword in hand;
Long time the manxome foe he sought—
So rested he by the Tumtum tree
And stood awhile in thought.

"The Raven" / **By Edgar Allen Poe**

Once upon a midnight dreary, while I pondered, weak and weary,
Over many a quaint and curious volume of forgotten lore—
While I nodded, nearly napping, suddenly there came a tapping,
As of some one gently rapping, rapping at my chamber door.
"'Tis some visitor," I muttered, "tapping at my chamber door—
Only this and nothing more."

"She Walks in Beauty" / **Lord Byron**

She walks in beauty, like the night
Of cloudless climes and starry skies;
And all that's best of dark and bright
Meet in her aspect and her eyes;
Thus mellowed to that tender light
Which heaven to gaudy day denies.

One shade the more, one ray the less,
Had half impaired the nameless grace
Which waves in every raven tress,
Or softly lightens o'er her face;
Where thoughts serenely sweet express,
How pure, how dear their dwelling-place.

And on that cheek, and o'er that brow,
So soft, so calm, yet eloquent,
The smiles that win, the tints that glow,
But tell of days in goodness spent,
A mind at peace with all below,
A heart whose love is innocent!

"The Gettysburg Address" / By Abraham Lincoln

Four score and seven years ago our fathers brought forth on this continent, a new nation, conceived in Liberty, and dedicated to the proposition that all men are created equal.

Now we are engaged in a great civil war, testing whether that nation, or any nation so conceived and so dedicated, can long endure. We are met on a great battle-field of that war. We have come to dedicate a portion of that field, as a final resting place for those who here gave their lives that that nation might live. It is altogether fitting and proper that we should do this.

But, in a larger sense, we can not dedicate -- we can not consecrate -- we can not hallow -- this ground. The brave men, living and dead, who struggled here, have consecrated it, far above our poor power to add or detract. The world will little note, nor long remember what we say here, but it can never forget what they did here. It is for us the living, rather, to be dedicated here to the unfinished work which they who fought here have thus far so nobly advanced. It is rather for us to be here dedicated to the great task remaining before us -- that from these honored dead we take increased devotion to that cause for which they gave the last full measure of devotion -- that we here highly resolve that these dead shall not have died in vain -- that this nation, under God, shall have a new birth of freedom -- and that government of the people, by the people, for the people, shall not perish from the earth.

Selection from "I Have a Dream" / By Martin Luther King, Jr.

I have a dream that one day every valley shall be exalted, and every hill and mountain shall be made low, the rough places will be made plain, and the crooked places will be made straight, and the glory of the Lord shall be revealed and all flesh shall see it together.

This is our hope. This is the faith that I go back to the South with. With this faith we will be able to hew out of the mountain of despair a stone of hope. With this faith we will be able to transform the jangling discords of our nation into a beautiful symphony of brotherhood. With this faith we will be able to work together, to pray together, to struggle together, to go to jail together, to stand up for freedom together, knowing that we will be free one day.

This will be the day, this will be the day when all of God's children will be able to sing with new meaning "My country 'tis of thee, sweet land of liberty, of thee I sing. Land where my father's died, land of the Pilgrim's pride, from every mountainside, let freedom ring!"

Selection from Tillsbury Speech / Queen Elizabeth I

My loving people,

We have been persuaded by some that are careful of our safety to take heed how we commit ourselves to armed multitudes, for fear of treachery. But I assure you, I do not desire to live to distrust my faithful and loving people.

Let tyrants fear. I have always so behaved myself that, under God, I have placed my chiefest strength and safeguard in the loyal hearts and good-will of my subjects; and therefore I am come amongst you, as you see, at this time, not for my recreation and disport, but being resolved, in the midst and heat of the battle, to live and die amongst you all; to lay down for my God, and for my kingdom, and my people, my honour and my blood, even in the dust.

I know I have the body of a weak and feeble woman; but I have the heart and stomach of a king, and of a king of England too, and think foul scorn that Parma or Spain, or any prince of Europe, should dare to invade the borders of my realm: to which rather than any dishonour shall grow by me, I myself will take up arms, I myself will be your general, judge, and rewarder of every one of your virtues in the field.

I know already, for your forwardness you have deserved rewards and crowns; and We do assure you on a word of a prince, they shall be duly paid. In the mean time, my lieutenant general shall be in my stead, than whom never prince commanded a more noble or worthy subject; not doubting but by your obedience to my general, by your concord in the camp, and your valour in the field, we shall shortly have a famous victory over these enemies of my God, of my kingdom, and of my people.

Selection from Inaugural Address / John F. Kennedy

"In the long history of the world, only a few generations have been granted the role of defending freedom in its hour of maximum danger. I do not shrink from this responsibility–I welcome it. I do not believe that any of us would exchange places with any other people or any other generation. The energy, the faith, the devotion which we bring to this endeavor will light our country and all who serve it–and the glow from that fire can truly light the world.

And so, my fellow Americans: ask not what your country can do for you–ask what you can do for your country.

My fellow citizens of the world: ask not what America will do for you, but what together we can do for the freedom of man.

Finally, whether you are citizens of America or citizens of the world, ask of us here the same high standards of strength and sacrifice which we ask of you. With a good conscience our only sure reward, with history the final judge of our deeds, let us go forth to lead the land

Selection from "Atoms for Peace" / Dwight D. Eisenhower

To pause there would be to confirm the hopeless finality of a belief that two atomic colossi are doomed malevolently uh to eye each other indefinitely across a trembling world. To stop there would be to accept hope-helplessly*, the probability of civilization destroyed, the annihilation of the irreplaceable heritage of mankind handed down to us generation from generation, and the condemnation of mankind to begin all over again, the age-old struggle upward from savagery toward decency and right and justice. Surely no sane member of the human race could discover victory in such desolation.

Could anyone wish his name to be coupled by history with such human degradation and destruction? Occasional pages of history do record the faces of the "great destroyers," but the whole book of history reveals mankind's never-ending quest for peace and mankind's God-given capacity to build.

It is with the book of history, and not with isolated pages, that the United States will ever wish to be identified. My country wants to be constructive, not destructive. It wants agreements, not wars, among nations. It wants itself to live in freedom and in the confidence that the people of every other nation enjoy equally the right of choosing their own way of life.

So my country's purpose is to help us move out of the dark chamber of horrors into the light, to find a way by which the minds of men, the hopes of men, the souls of men everywhere, can move forward toward peace and happiness and well-being.

Selection from "Their Finest Hour" / By Winston Churchill

What General Weygand called the Battle of France is over. I expect that the Battle of Britain is about to begin. Upon this battle depends the survival of Christian civilization. Upon it depends our own British life, and the long continuity of our institutions and our Empire. The whole fury and might of the enemy must very soon be turned on us.

Hitler knows that he will have to break us in this Island or lose the war. If we can stand up to him, all Europe may be free and the life of the world may move forward into broad, sunlit uplands. But if we fail, then the whole world, including the United States, including all that we have known and cared for, will sink into the abyss of a new Dark Age made more sinister, and perhaps more protracted, by the lights of perverted science.

Let us therefore brace ourselves to our duties, and so bear ourselves that if the British Empire and its Commonwealth last for a thousand years, men will still say, 'This was their finest hour.'

Selection from "The Struggle for Human Rights" / **Eleanor Roosevelt**

I have come this evening to talk with you on one of the greatest issues of our time -- that is the preservation of human freedom. I have chosen to discuss it here in France, at the Sorbonne, because here in this soil the roots of human freedom have long ago struck deep and here they have been richly nourished. It was here the Declaration of the Rights of Man was proclaimed, and the great slogans of the French Revolution -- liberty, equality, fraternity -- fired the imagination of men. I have chosen to discuss this issue in Europe because this has been the scene of the greatest historic battles between freedom and tyranny. I have chosen to discuss it in the early days of the General Assembly because the issue of human liberty is decisive for the settlement of outstanding political differences and for the future of the United Nations.

It is my belief, and I am sure it is also yours, that the struggle for democracy and freedom is a critical struggle, for their preservation is essential to the great objective of the United Nations to maintain international peace and security. Among free men the end cannot justify the means. We know the patterns of totalitarianism -- the single political party, the control of schools, press, radio, the arts, the sciences, and the church to support autocratic authority; these are the age-old patterns against which men have struggled for three thousand years. These are the signs of reaction, retreat, and retrogression. The United Nations must hold fast to the heritage of freedom won by the struggle of its people; it must help us to pass it on to generations to come.

The development of the ideal of freedom and its translation into the everyday life of the people in great areas of the earth is the product of the efforts of many peoples. It is the fruit of a long tradition of vigorous thinking and courageous action. No one race and on one people can claim to have done all the work to achieve greater dignity for human beings and great freedom to develop human personality. In each generation and in each country there must be a continuation of the struggle and new steps forward must be taken since this is preeminently a field in which to stand still is to retreat.

Glossary of Terms

A

Active voice: A sentence in which the subject is doing the action of the verb.

Advance Organizer: A brief list of the main points you will use to prove the claim of your thesis. It is often presented as a list within the thesis statement but can also be its own sentence directly after the thesis.

Adverb: Words that modify verbs, adjectives, or other adverbs.

Alphanumeric Outline: A type of outline that lists the key information under various letters and numbers to show how the points and evidence will be arranged.

Ambiguous: Something that is vague or unclear and therefore can have more than one meaning.

Analysis: An explanation of the evidence and how it supports the claim.

Anecdote: A very brief story that is interesting or amusing in some way.

Attributive adjective: A descriptive word that comes directly before the noun it describes.

Antecedent: The noun that the pronoun refers to.

B

Background Information: Information that the reader needs in order to understand the general topic of the essay more clearly.

Body Paragraph: A paragraph that presents one main point to prove the thesis of your essay.

Brackets: The symbol [ ] used to show that a word was added to the original quotation to allow it to be grammatically correct.

Brainstorming Web: A visual way of writing down your ideas in which you place the main idea at the center of your web and list many connected ideas off of that.

C

Citation: A mention of the source where you read, heard, or saw the information you are referencing.

Claim: A main point from your thesis that you are arguing for in a particular paragraph.

Clause: A group of words with a subject and a verb.

Cliché: A phrase or expression that is so overused that it is no longer interesting.

Clincher: The final sentence of the conclusion paragraph that is memorable and provides a send off to the reader.

Complement: Something that pairs with another in order to enhance them both; i.e. complementary colors.

Complex Sentence: A dependent clause connected to an independent clause using a subordinating conjunction.

Compound Sentence: Two independent clauses connected together with a comma and a coordinating conjunction to form one sentence.

Compound-Complex Sentence: A sentence containing three total clauses. Two of the clauses are joined by a coordinating conjunction and two are joined by a subordinating conjunction.

Conclusion: The last paragraph of an essay that sums up everything that was stated and provides a sense of closure to the essay.

Connotation: The feeling associated with a word that goes beyond its literal dictionary definition.

Contraction: Two words reduced to one through use of the apostrophe, i.e. *can't, it's, we've*, etc.

Coordinating Conjunction: A word such as "and," "but," or "or," that connects words, phrases, or sentences of equal importance.

Counterargument: An argument that goes against the main claim of the essay.

D

Dependent Clause: Also know as a subordinating clause, this is a clause that begins with a subordinating conjunction and cannot stand by itself.

Descriptive essay: An essay written to paint a clear picture for the reader.

E

Ellipsis: A The symbol of three periods in a row to show that a word or words have been left out of a direct quotation.

Essay: A piece of work that discusses one main topic. It begins with an introduction and ends with a conclusion.

Essay Map: This is a visual way to chart out the main points and their corresponding support points before writing an essay.

Evidence: Information that supports your claim. It could include facts, statistics, personal experience, etc.

F

Figurative language: Using words in a way that goes beyond their literal dictionary definitions.

First Person Pronouns: Pronouns directed at the audience your are speaking to. It includes the pronouns "you," "your," and "yours."

Figurative Language: Using words in a way that goes beyond their literal dictionary definitions.

G

Gerund: A word formed from a verb that acts at a noun in a sentence.

H

Homonyms: Two words that are spelled and pronounced the same but have different meanings.

Hook: A catchy opener that makes your audience interested in your essay and encourages them to continue reading.

I

ICE: A method of incorporating quotes or paraphrase where you introduced, cite, and explain the information.

Indent: Moving the beginning of a line to the right about half an inch. When typing this is done by pressing the tab key once or the space bar 7-10 times.

Independent Clause: A clause that makes sense by itself. Any simple sentence is an independent clause.

Imperative Sentence: A sentence that makes a command and uses the implied pronoun "you."

Interrogative Sentence: A sentence that asks a question.

In-text citations: Citations in the body of the essay that shows the reader which source each fact or idea came from.

Introduction: The first paragraph of an essay that grabs the reader's attention and presents what the essay is about. It begins with the hook and ends with the thesis.

M

Metaphor: A figure of speech where one thing is stated to be another different thing without using *like* or *as*.

O

Onomatopoeia: A word that represents and reflects a certain sound.

Outline: A document that provides a clear map of each paragraph of an essay by listing the key information under various letters and numbers to show how the points and evidence will be arranged in the essay.

P

Paragraph: A group of sentences with one central theme.

Parallel Language: Using the same part of speech and structure for each item, phrase, or clause in a list within a single sentence.

Paraphrase: Information from a source that you wrote in your own words and sentence structure.

Participial Phrase: A group of words that begins with either the past or present participle, followed by an object that goes with it. It always functions as an adjective.

Passive voice: A sentence where the subject is receiving the action of the verb.

Participle: A word that comes from a verb but is used as an adjective. It is also combined with helping verbs to form certain tenses.

Peer-reviewed: An article that has been checked by experts to verify the facts and quality of the article.

Personification: Giving human traits to nonhuman objects or creatures.

Plagiarism: An act of academic dishonesty where you do not give proper credit to the source of your information, or you give credit but do not properly quote or paraphrase.

Predicate adjective: A descriptive word that follows a linking verb but describes the subject.

Preposition: Words that tell the relationship between a noun (the object of the preposition) and another word in the sentence.

Prepositional Phrase: A group of words beginning with a preposition and ending with the object of that preposition.

Prewriting: The process of coming up with and writing down ideas relating to a topic in preparation for writing an essay or similar piece of work.

Print Source: Items found in a physical print format.

Prompt: The directions of an essay assignment that provides a question to answer or other guidance on what to write about.

Pronoun: A word that takes the place of a noun or noun phrase.

Persuasive Essay: An essay written to convince the reader to do or believe something.

Q

Quotation: A passage taken verbatim (word-for-word) from a source around which you place quotation marks.

R

Rebuttal: A response disproving or weakening the reasons against the main claim of the essay.

Research: The process of investigating and learning more about a topic through books, lectures, videos, and journals.

Research databases: Searchable collections of information online, especially journal articles.

S

Search Engine: A program into which you type key terms and receive back Internet results related to those terms.

Second Person Pronouns: Pronouns directed at the audience your are speaking to. It includes the pronouns "you," "your," and "yours."

Sensory detail: Information that triggers one of the five senses: taste, touch, sight, smell, and sound.

Simile: A figure of speech using *like* or *as* to compare two seemingly unrelated things.

Stream of Consciousness: Writing or speaking as the thoughts come to you with no particular order or organization.

Subordinating Clause: *See Dependent Clause*

Subordinating Conjunction: A conjunction like "because" or "since" that begins a dependent clause.

T

Tabloids: Magazines or newspapers that capture people's attention with sensational headlines and are notorious for containing inaccurate or exaggerated information or information taken out of context.

Thesaurus: A book that lists words with their synonyms grouped together.

Thesis statement: One to two sentences that present the claim that you plan to argue for in your essay. It should clearly identify the topic, your point of view, and the main ways you plan to prove or explain that point of view.

Topic Sentence: Also known as a claim, this sentence is the first sentence of a body paragraph that provides the main point that you will be arguing for in the paragraph.

Transitions: Words or phrases such as "next" or "on the other hand" that help the reader move from one sentence or idea to the next.

V

Verbatim: The exact same words that were used in an original passage.

W

Works cited page: A page included at the end of your essay that lists all the sources you used in your research, formatted in a particular way.

Wrap-up: The last sentence in a body paragraph that gives a sense of closure to the paragraph. It may also provide a transition into the next main point.

THALES PRESS
Thales Academy
DEVELOPING CLASSICAL THINKERS
THALES COLLEGE

Made in the USA
Columbia, SC
17 May 2025